HEY KIDS
COLOR
ME IN!

GOING TO
DISNEYLAND

A GUIDE FOR KIDS & KIDS AT ♥

by Shannon W. Laskey

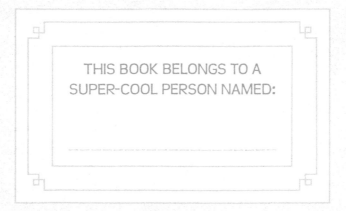

THIS BOOK BELONGS TO A
SUPER-COOL PERSON NAMED:

Orchard Hill Press

This book is dedicated
to my two sons

Edward & Clark

A.K.A. my two favorite people
to go to Disneyland with!
You both are just like storybook heroes
—handsome, strong, brave and good.
I love you guys!

xoxo,
Ma

A Note to Grown-Ups

When my oldest son was seven, we were planning a trip to Disneyland. I headed to the kids' section of the old Lafayette library to get him a guidebook for kids about the park and was so surprised to find out that they didn't have any! Not only that but, when I looked into it further, I couldn't find any at all. Sure, there were guidebooks about how to go to Disneyland WITH kids but nothing FOR kids. Being an illustrator, graphic designer, writer and Disney devotee, I knew I had my next project.

As I was writing the book, a fellow Disney fan shared an interesting theory with me. She said that if you go to Disneyland as a child, you will always have a magical feeling about it—and if you go for your first time as an adult, you'll never quite understand what all the fuss is about. I was three when I first visited Disneyland and my most vivid memory was being absolutely thrilled riding Pirates of the Caribbean. I thought the pirates were *really* firing cannons over our heads!

To me, Disneyland is the most special Disney park—not only because I went there when I was young but because it's the one Walt Disney himself created. He was so successful because he never lost that sense of wonder about the world that every child has. It's so cool that we can visit Disneyland, walk in his footsteps, experience the things he himself oversaw and recapture that wondrous joy of childhood that he knew so well.

If you are giving this book to a child, I hope it enhances their visit—and yours—and helps them enjoy a lifelong, nostalgic glow each time they return to the park. If you're an adult reader with no kids in sight, I warmly welcome you! I hope you enjoy this book —and Disneyland—just as much as the kids do. Have a magical time!

xoxo,
Shannon

We're going to Disneyland
-please note the Tink lining!

ABOUT THE AUTHOR
Shannon W. Laskey is a freelance illustrator, graphic designer and writer. This is the second book that she's written and illustrated but the first that she's written, illustrated AND designed. Shannon lives with her husband, two sons and two chickens in Northern California much, much too far away from Disneyland.

Edited, Proofread, Fact Checked and Fine-Tooth Combed by Hugh Allison

Front cover and spine illustrations by Shannon W. Laskey
Front cover and spine photographs by Dave DeCaro
Back cover illustration by Kirsten Ulve • Back cover caricature by Rolly Crump

LEGAL MUMBO JUMBO	WHAT IT MEANS
No part of this publication may be reproduced, distributed or transmitted in any form or by any means, including photocopying, recording or other electronic or mechanical methods, without the prior written consent of the author, except in the case of brief quotations in critical reviews and certain other non-commercial uses permitted by copyright law.	Don't copy this book, okay?
This book is neither authorized nor sponsored nor endorsed by the Disney Company or its subsidiaries. It is an unofficial and unauthorized book, and not a Disney product.	This book is NOT made by Disney!
All products, services and mentions of names and places associated with the Disney Company, its businesses and other companies independent of the Disney Company are not intended to infringe on any existing copyrights or registered trademarks of their respective companies, but are used in context for educational purposes.	The stuff talked about in this book is owned by other people. We're just telling you about it.
The opinions and statements expressed in the quotations and text are solely the opinions of those people who are quoted and do not necessarily reflect the opinions and policies of the Disney Company and its subsidiaries nor the author or the publisher.	The quotes in this book are what the person who said it thought and might not be what Disney, the author or the publisher thinks.
While every precaution has been taken in the preparation of this book, no responsibility is taken by the author or the publisher for errors or omissions. Neither is any liability assumed for damages resulting, or alleged to result, directly or indirectly from the use of the information contained herein.	We tried not to make any mistakes while writing this book but if we did, well, these things happen. (But if we did, we're sorry!) (And if you notice something that's a mistake, will you let us know?)

Printed in the United States of America
ISBN #978-0-9912954-3-2
Orchard Hill Press

For more information on Orchard Hill Press, visit www.OrchardHillPress.com
For more information on Going To Guides, visit www.GoingToGuides.com

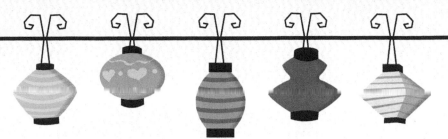

Table of Contents

How did Disneyland get started? Find out here!

Info on the whole park

Disneyland's 8 themed lands

Detailed list of what's in this book

Know the stories before you ride the rides!

Disneyland Dictionary

Here are some Disneyland words and phrases to know before you go:

A

ATTRACTION—Things at the park to see, do or ride are called attractions. These can be anything from a treehouse to a live show to a roller coaster.

AUDIO-ANIMATRONIC—Disneyland has Audio-Animatronic figures in many attractions. These are a type of robot that moves and makes sounds but stays fixed in one spot. *More about Audio-Animatronics on page 42.*

C

CAST MEMBER—In a play or movie, the performers are called the cast. The people who work in Disneyland are performing their jobs for the park's visitors, so they are called Cast Members. *More about Cast Members on page 24.*

F

FASTPASS—Many of the more popular things to do in Disneyland use FastPass. You'll get a specific time to return without having to wait in a long line. There is still a line for FastPass holders but it will usually be much shorter than the regular one. *More about FastPass on page 27.*

G

GUEST—Disneyland calls its visitors Guests and loves to make them feel special. If you ever have to sign for something in Disneyland, Cast Members will ask for your autograph instead of your signature.

H

HIDDEN MICKEY—When the shape of Mickey Mouse is used in the designs of attractions and other spots, it's called a Hidden Mickey. Some of these shapes are very easy to find and others are very difficult. There are hundreds of Hidden Mickeys in Disneyland! *More about Hidden Mickeys on page 40.*

I

IMAGINEER—This term is a combination of the words "imagination" and "engineer." It describes the talented people who create the magic in Disneyland. They design and oversee every detail, from the machinery that will make a ride work right down to the pattern of the wallpaper inside a restaurant.

Special Stuff in This Book

Look out for these handy dandy symbols and features!

The **Hot Tip** symbol is found near insider info that not just everyone knows about.

Eye Spy symbols let you know about special things to spy with your little eye.

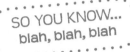

These **So You Know** areas explain a little bit more about words or phrases you might not know, like "live-action," "raja," and "bayou."

This **stamp** tells you what type of attraction it is, what year it opened in Disneyland and what it's like. Slower attractions are "Calm & Mellow," faster attractions are "Wild & Thrilling" and the ones that are somewhere in between are "Lively & Exciting."

The smiley **Fun Fact** symbol is found near extra tidbits of fun and fascinating trivia.

If you love to color, you may enjoy coloring in the **black-and-white images** in this book. Sharp colored pencils or colored ballpoint pens will work best.

There's a **scrapbook** on pages 166–169. While you're in Disneyland, save any tags, receipts, tickets and other flat things so you can add them to the scrapbook later.

The fun doesn't have to stop because you're standing in line. Play **Waiting Games** when you're waiting for a ride, sitting in a restaurant or just taking a break. Time flies when you're having fun.

MAY BE SCARY

This **caution** sign near the name of an attraction means that some people find it scary. If you're unsure, ask a Cast Member what to expect.

★ ★ ★ ★ ★ ★ ★ ★ ★ ★ A WORD TO THE WISE ★ ★ ★ ★ ★ ★ ★ ★ ★ ★

There are lots of activities, games and fill-in-the-blank areas in this book. A ballpoint pen or pencil will work best. Don't use markers because the ink might bleed through to the other side of the page.

Sleeping Beauty Castle shimmers behind the *Partners* statue of Walt Disney and Mickey Mouse by Disney Imagineer Blaine Gibson.

Disney's Land

What Will You Find in This Chapter?

Once Upon a Time...

Not so very long ago in Anaheim, California there was a peaceful grove of orange trees. Today that land is the home to one of the world's most beloved theme parks called—you guessed it—Disneyland! But how did it all come to be? Who created this wonderful place? Where does the name come from? Disneyland is named after the man who dreamed it all up: Walter Elias Disney.

★ Meet Walt Disney

Walt Disney was born in Illinois way-y-y back on December 5th, 1901 and spent his childhood in the Midwest. Little Walt loved to draw and sold pictures to his neighbors. Later he was a cartoonist for his school paper. At 16 years old, Walt joined the Red Cross during the First World War and drove an ambulance in France—which he covered in doodles! After coming back home to America, Walt worked at an art studio, an advertising agency and his own animation studio before moving to sunny California to start a new company with his big brother Roy.

Photograph by Hart Preston/The LIFE Picture Collection/Getty Images

TIME MACHINE

1901
It's a boy! Walter Elias Disney is born on Dec. 5th in Chicago, Illinois & is the fourth of five children.

1923
Walt & his brother Roy create Disney Brothers Cartoon Studio in California, later renamed The Walt Disney Studios.

1928
Mickey is an instant hit when "Steamboat Willie" is released on Nov. 18th, now considered Mickey's birthday.

1937
Heigh-ho! Disney's "Snow White & the Seven Dwarfs" is the world's first full-length animated movie.

★ A Mouse is Born

SO YOU KNOW... **newsreels** = short movies about news & events

Walt Disney's first big success was Mickey Mouse. He had created other successful cartoons for other companies but wanted to make a character all his own. Walt sketched out a cute little Mouse in shorts. Legend has it that he wanted to call the little fellow "Mortimer Mouse", but his wife thought that sounded snooty and suggested "Mickey" instead. Back then, movie theaters would show **newsreels** and short cartoons first, even if it wasn't a movie for kids. In 1928, audiences were shown the first cartoon ever to have sound effects that went along with the action—or synchronized sound—and they LOVED it! That cartoon was Steamboat Willie starring Mickey and Minnie Mouse. Later, Disney created more cartoons with new friends for Mickey and Minnie, like Pluto, Goofy and Donald Duck!

HOT TIP You can watch *Steamboat Willie* and other **vintage Disney cartoons** in the Main Street Cinema in Disneyland! *More info on page 46.*

> "I only hope that we never lose sight of one thing—that it was all started by a mouse."
> — WALT DISNEY

FUN FACT
When making those early cartoons, sound effects had to be recorded live in one try. If someone messed up, they had to start all over & make a new recording.

YIKES!

OOPS!

CLACK! CLACK!

DARN it, LES!

Lucky Thirteen!

Disneyland's address, 1313 Disneyland Drive, is code for **Mickey Mouse**. "M" is the thirteenth letter in the alphabet so the numbers "1313" stand for "MM" or Mickey Mouse! What would **YOUR** initials be if you wrote them as numbers?

A = 1	H = 8	O = 15	V = 22
B = 2	I = 9	P = 16	W = 23
C = 3	J = 10	Q = 17	X = 24
D = 4	K = 11	R = 18	Y = 25
E = 5	L = 12	S = 19	Z = 26
F = 6	M = 13	T = 20	
G = 7	N = 14	U = 21	

1955
Disneyland Park opens with five lands: Adventureland, Fantasyland, Frontierland, Main Street USA & Tomorrowland.

1961
Walt Disney founds the first university for visual & performing arts, the California Institute of the Arts—or CalArts.

1966
Walt Disney dies of lung cancer. Rumor has it that the last words he wrote were "Kurt Russell."

1967
The last ride Walt Disney worked on opens: Pirates of the Caribbean.

★ At the Movies

Walt Disney liked to dream big so he decided that The Walt Disney Studios would make the world's first full-length **animated** movie: Snow White and the Seven Dwarfs. Most people thought he was crazy and called the project Disney's Folly because they thought it was a foolish idea. But when the movie came out it was a HUGE hit and took the world by storm! A critic for the *New York Times* called it one of the ten best movies of the year. Thirteen years later in 1950, the studio released their first **live-action** movie, Treasure Island. Today, The Walt Disney Studios and the companies they own have made hundreds and hundreds of animated and live-action movies—maybe you've seen a few?

FUN FACT

The 750 artists working on "Snow White & the Seven Dwarfs" created over 2 million drawings, & the finished movie had over 250,000 separate pictures! There were NO computers & it was all done by hand.

I MEAN, WOW!

"We don't make movies to make money. We make money to make more movies."
—WALT DISNEY

DISNEY THROUGH THE DECADES

Disney started making animated movies way back in the 1930s! Put a ✔ next to the ones you've seen. Just so you know, this is **not** even all of them!

1930s:
☐ Snow White & the Seven Dwarfs

1940s:
☐ Pinocchio ☐ Fantasia ☐ Dumbo ☐ Bambi
☐ The Adventures of Ichabod & Mister Toad

1950s:
☐ Cinderella ☐ Alice in Wonderland ☐ Peter Pan
☐ Lady & the Tramp ☐ Sleeping Beauty

1960s:
☐ 101 Dalmatians ☐ The Sword in the Stone
☐ The Jungle Book

> "It's kind of fun to do the impossible."
> —WALT DISNEY

★ Good Clean Fun

As Walt Disney's career grew, so did his family. He and his wife Lillian had two daughters named Diane and Sharon. The girls loved to ride the merry-go-round at Griffith Park in Los Angeles. One day as Walt was sitting on a bench watching them, he had an idea for a different kind of place—a place where kids and parents could have fun together. He had visited several small amusement parks, carnivals and circuses but he felt like they were all kind of rundown and dirty. He dreamed of a place that would be clean and beautiful where all the visitors would be treated like first-class guests. In 1953, Walt bought land in Anaheim, CA for Mickey Mouse Park. Later the name changed to Disneylandia and then the name that stuck—Disneyland.

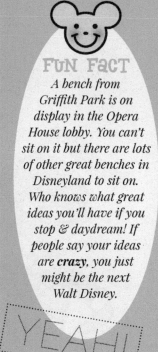

FUN FACT
A bench from Griffith Park is on display in the Opera House lobby. You can't sit on it but there are lots of other great benches in Disneyland to sit on. Who knows what great ideas you'll have if you stop & daydream! If people say your ideas are **crazy***, you just might be the next Walt Disney.*

YEAH!!

1970s:
☐ The Aristocats   ☐ Robin Hood   ☐ Winnie the Pooh   ☐ The Rescuers

1980s:
☐ The Fox & the Hound   ☐ The Black Cauldron
☐ The Great Mouse Detective   ☐ Oliver & Company   ☐ The Little Mermaid

1990s:
☐ The Rescuers Down Under   ☐ Beauty & the Beast   ☐ Aladdin
☐ The Lion King   ☐ Pocahontas   ☐ The Hunchback of Notre Dame
☐ Hercules   ☐ Mulan   ☐ Tarzan

2000s:
☐ Dinosaur   ☐ The Emperor's New Groove   ☐ Atlantis: The Lost Empire
☐ Lilo & Stitch   ☐ Treasure Planet   ☐ Brother Bear
☐ Home on the Range   ☐ Chicken Little   ☐ Meet the Robinsons   ☐ Bolt
☐ The Princess & the Frog

2010s:
☐ Tangled   ☐ Wreck-It Ralph   ☐ Frozen   ☐ Big Hero 6

What's your favorite TV show?

Disneyland!

Where's your family going on vacation?

Disneyland!

What's your dog's name?

Disneyland!

★ Disneyland TV

Walt Disney told a lot of people his idea for Disneyland and most of them thought he was crazy. He was used to that so he just ignored them! It took him a long time to get enough money to build the park. To help pay for it, he made a weekly TV show called Disneyland that showed the park being built. Though Walt had been working on the idea for over ten years, it only took one year to actually build Disneyland. ABC-TV's broadcast from Disneyland on Opening Day was the biggest live **telecast** in history!

Disney Worldwide

If you want to visit **EVERY** Disney park there is, here's your checklist:

CALIFORNIA
- ☐ Disneyland Park
- ☐ Disney California Adventure Park

FLORIDA
- ☐ Magic Kingdom
- ☐ Epcot
- ☐ Disney's Hollywood Studios
- ☐ Disney's Animal Kingdom
- ☐ Disney's Typhoon Lagoon Water Park
- ☐ Disney's Blizzard Beach Water Park

TOKYO
- ☐ Tokyo Disneyland
- ☐ Tokyo DisneySea

PARIS
- ☐ Disneyland Park, Paris
- ☐ Walt Disney Studios Park

HONG KONG
- ☐ Hong Kong Disneyland

SHANGHAI (opening Spring 2016)
- ☐ Shanghai Disneyland

"To all who come to this happy place: welcome. Disneyland is your land."
—WALT DISNEY

This vintage photo is from July 18, 1955—the first day Disneyland was open to the public.

★ Opening Day

Disneyland's Opening Day celebration was on Sunday, July 17th, 1955. Ten thousand lucky VIPs were invited for a preview of the park but—uh oh—more than twenty thousand extra people showed up! In fact, there were many challenges that day. Many of the drinking fountains were not working yet, streets that were newly paved were sticky, and some areas had to close while a gas leak was fixed. Worst of all, the weather was a mega hot and steamy 110 degrees! Not one to give up, Walt opened the park to the public the very next day as planned. By the next year, over five million people had visited Disneyland. These days Disneyland is so popular it welcomes over 16.7 million Guests every year and is one of the TOP vacation destinations in the whole world!

DISNEYLAND IN 1955	DISNEYLAND IN 2015
★ Under 2-dozen attractions	★ Over 60 attractions
★ 5 lands	★ 8 lands
★ Closed seasonally 1 day a week	★ Open every day, all year round
★ Pay for admission AND ride tickets	★ Admission ticket includes all rides

★ Ticket Talk

When Disneyland first opened, admission tickets were just one dollar for adults and fifty cents for kids BUT you paid extra depending on which attractions you wanted to do. A few months later, they started selling tickets for attractions instead but not everything used the same kind. There were A, B, C, D and E tickets. The newest and most popular attractions used an E-ticket which cost the most money. People started calling anything that was special or thrilling an "E Ticket." A famous example of this was when astronaut Sally Ride—the first American woman launched into space—said, "Ever been to Disneyland? That was definitely an E ticket!" In 1982, Disney got rid of the separate attraction tickets and Guests paid one price to enter with attractions included.

Whee! This is a real E-ticket ride!

Actually, this is a B-ticket ride!

> "Disneyland will never be completed. It will continue to grow as long as there is imagination left in the world."
> —WALT DISNEY

★ New & Improved

Disneyland is always changing. Sometimes little things change like the flowers that are used to form the shape of Mickey Mouse's head at the Main Entrance and sometimes big things change like a ride is removed to make room for something brand new. Over half of the attractions that were there when the park opened are still around today but there have been hundreds of rides, shows, shops, restaurants and exhibits that have come and gone. Enjoy your visit to Disneyland—it may not be the same when you go back!

PHony BaLoney!

All of these used to be in Disneyland —except for **one**. Can you put a ✓ next to the fake? *Answer on page 181.*

☐ Aluminum Hall of Fame

☐ Bathroom of Tomorrow

☐ The Beast's Beauty Shop

☐ Chicken of the Sea Restaurant

☐ The Intimate Apparel Shop

☐ Main Street Flower Mart

☐ Mike Fink Keel Boats

☐ The Mile Long Bar

☐ Rainbow Ridge Pack Mules

R.I.P.
SOME ATTRACTIONS THAT ARE GONERS

1955–1959
Conestoga Wagons
Horse-drawn wagon ride through Frontierland along the Rivers of America

1956–1994
Skyway
Suspended gondolas carried Guests between Tomorrowland station and Fantasyland station (you can still see the Fantasyland station behind the trees near Casey Jr. Circus Train)

1957–1958
Viewliner
Miniature train traveled through parts of Fantasyland and Tomorrowland

1957–1993
Motor Boat Cruise
Motor boats embarked from a covered loading platform—now the site of a rest spot near Edelweiss Snacks

1962–1982
Big Game Safari Shooting Gallery
Jungle-themed shooting gallery —now the site of Indiana Jones Adventure Outpost

1967–1985
Adventure Thru Inner Space
Riders were shrunk to a microscopic size —now the site of Star Tours

1972–2001
Country Bear Jamboree
Audio-Animatronic animals sang traditional American folk songs—now the site of The Many Adventures of Winnie the Pooh

1974–1988
America Sings
Audio-Animatronic animals sang patriotic American songs —now the site of Tomorrowland Expo Center

Disneyland's crown jewel, Sleeping Beauty Castle, is an original attraction and still pretty in pink after 60 years!

VISITING DISNEYLAND

What Will You Find in This Chapter?

MAP of tHE DiSNEYLAND RESORT

KEY
- ⬤ FOOD & DRINKS
- ⬤ HOTELS
- ⬤ MOVIE THEATER
- ⬤ PARKS
- ⬤ SHOPS

Disneyland

Downtown Disney

Disneyland Hotel

Disney's Grand Californian Hotel & Spa

Disney's Paradise Pier Hotel

Disney California Adventure

Disneyland Today

You're going to Disneyland?! That is SO exciting! Whether this visit will be your first or your hundred-and-first, it's sure to be a big adventure full of fun and excitement. When Disneyland first opened in 1955, there was only Disneyland and—about three months later—the Disneyland Hotel. Today everything is bigger and better and the whole area is now called the Disneyland Resort. There's a second theme park called Disney California Adventure, shops and restaurants in Downtown Disney and two more Disney hotels—Paradise Pier and Grand Californian. With all there is to see and do, many people come and visit for more than one day!

 HOT TIP Wear comfy shoes. The average Disneyland Resort visitor walks over **five miles a day!**

★ 8 Themed Lands

Disneyland has different sections called lands and each has its own theme and unique look. If you've already been to Disneyland, put a ✓ by your fave! If you've never ever been to Disneyland, put a ✓ by the land you think you'll like best just from reading the name—then turn the page to see what the lands are all about!

☐ Adventureland   ☐ Critter Country   ☐ Fantasyland
☐ Frontierland   ☐ Main Street USA   ☐ Mickey's Toontown
☐ New Orleans Square ☐ Tomorrowland

Disneyland's Lands

Critter Country
Sit and stay awhile in this woodsy setting. Splash down a steep mountainside, help paddle a 35-foot canoe & visit a friendly Pooh bear!

New Orleans Square
Delight in elegant splendor inspired by the French Quarter in New Orleans, Louisiana. Wander through charming courtyards, dare to enter a haunted house & brave pirate-infested waters!

Main Street USA
Enjoy the old-fashioned small-town charm of turn-of-the-century America. Catch free cartoons, enjoy a ride on an old-fashioned vehicle & browse through shops filled with candy, costumes & toys!

Fantasyland
Stroll through an enchanting village with quaint cottages & castles from the pages of your favorite storybooks. Discover a miniature town, meet beloved characters & ride a flying elephant!

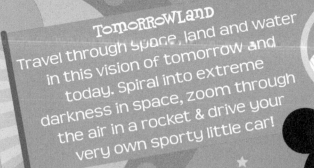

TOMORROWLAND
Travel through space, land and water in this vision of tomorrow and today. Spiral into extreme darkness in space, zoom through the air in a rocket & drive your very own sporty little car!

MICKEY'S TOONTOWN
Walk right into a cartoon in this area inspired by vintage animation & the movie *Who Framed Roger Rabbit*. See where Mickey & Minnie live, zip around on an inventive coaster & catch a spinning cab!

ADVENTURELAND
Travel far from civilization to the exotic, remote jungles of the South Pacific, Africa, Asia & South America. Claim your territory from the treetops & cruise a lush tropical river!

FRONTIERLAND
Step back in time to the days of the American Wild West. Roar past a dusty mining town on a runaway train, explore spooky caves & ride a majestic riverboat!

FUN FACT

*Disney's Magic
Kingdom in Florida
is much larger but
Disneyland has
MORE attractions.*

RAD!

★ So Much to See & Do

Disneyland has attractions, shops and restaurants. But wait, **there's more!** There are also live shows, bands, singers, dancers, parades, fireworks, seasonal events, characters to meet and special tours to take. When you walk in the Main Entrance, you can get a Map of the park and an Entertainment Times Guide with info on stage shows, live entertainment and character Meet n' Greets. The Entertainment Times Guide does NOT include info on everything that may be going on though. If you have questions about events—or anything else, head to City Hall in Main Street USA or ask a friendly Cast Member!

HOT TIP If you need a **map** or **guide** later in the day, ask inside a shop as they often have extras. **Street sweeper Cast Members** also carry maps and guides in their waist packs!

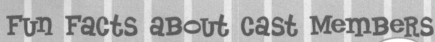

Fun Facts about Cast Members

New Cast Members have to go through training called "Disney University" to learn about the history of the Disney Company & all the rules about how they should look & act!

Cast Members make a point not to point. If you ask them where something is, they will use two fingers or their open hand to show you the way. Why? Pointing is considered rude in many international cultures!

Many Cast Members are never seen by the public. After closing time, a specially trained night crew work on repainting railings with a special paint that will dry overnight, replacing light bulbs before they burn out & much more!

Back in the early days, Cast Members were not allowed to have any facial hair even though Walt Disney himself had a mustache! Today it's okay —but visible tattoos, body piercings, long fingernails & wild hairstyles are all still a big no–no!

People come from all over the world to work for Disneyland & Cast Member name tags have the town they're from below their names. Take a look & you just might see someone from your town. It's a small world after all!

entertainment at a GLance

MAIN STREET USA

- Dapper Dans
- Disneyland Band
- The Hook & Ladder Co.
- Main Street Piano Player
- Pearly Band
- The Straw Hatters

FANTASYLAND

- Frozen
- Mickey and the Magical Map

TOMORROWLAND

- Jedi Training Academy
- Special Screenings

FRONTIERLAND

- Fantasmic!
- Farley the Fiddler
- The Laughing Stock Co.
- Mariachi Music

NEW ORLEANS SQUARE

- The Bootstrappers
- Jambalaya Jazz Band
- Royal Street Bachelors

MULTIPLE LANDS

- Disneyland Forever
- Mickey's Soundsational Parade
- Paint the Night

FiReWORKS & PaRaDes

DISNEYLAND FOREVER
images projected on buildings, narration, music and fireworks

BEST SEEN FROM:
Main Street USA
Matterhorn Mountain
Rivers of America

MICKEY'S SOUNDSATIONAL PARADE
Mickey leads a parade of floats, dancers and musicians

BEST SEEN FROM:
It's A Small World
Sleeping Beauty Castle
Town Square

PAINT THE NIGHT
Light-covered floats, dancers and music

BEST SEEN FROM:
It's A Small World
Sleeping Beauty Castle
Town Square

Just Some of the seasonal Fun

WINTER
- It's a Small World gets holiday decorations and a medley of Christmas music
- Jungle Cruise becomes Jingle Cruise with holiday-themed jokes and decorations
- New Year's Eve party hats, noisemakers, and fireworks at midnight

SPRING
- Valentine's Day decorations, treats and menus
- Mardi Gras beads, masks, music and treats in New Orleans Square
- Easter egg hunt and visits from the Easter Bunny

SUMMER
- Students from all over America perform in the All-American College Band
- Patriotic fireworks and U.S. Military marching bands celebrate the 4th of July
- Disneyland's Anniversary events take place before and on July 17th

FALL
- Halloween fun includes a carnival, Mickey's Halloween Party and trick-or-treating
- *The Nightmare Before Christmas* takes over Haunted Mansion
- Space Mountain becomes Space Mountain: Ghost Galaxy

attractions at a glance

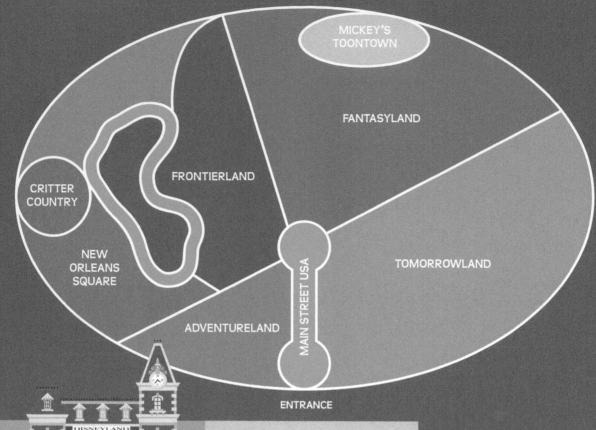

MICKEY'S
TOONTOWN

FANTASYLAND

CRITTER
COUNTRY

FRONTIERLAND

NEW
ORLEANS
SQUARE

TOMORROWLAND

MAIN STREET USA

ADVENTURELAND

ENTRANCE

DISNEYLAND

MAIN STREET USA
- Disney Gallery
- Disneyland Railroad
- Fire Station
- Great Moments with Mr. Lincoln
- Main Street Cinema
- Main Street Vehicles

MICKEY'S TOONTOWN
- Chip 'n Dale Treehouse
- Disneyland Railroad
- Donald's Boat
- Gadget's Go Coaster
- Goofy's Playhouse
- Mickey's House
- Minnie's House
- Roger Rabbit's Car Toon Spin

FRONTIERLAND
- Big Thunder
  Mountain Railroad
- Mark Twain Riverboat
- Pirate's Lair on
  Tom Sawyer Island
- Sailing Ship Columbia

NEW ORLEANS SQUARE
- Disneyland Railroad
- Haunted Mansion
- Pirates of the Caribbean

FANTASYLAND
- Alice in Wonderland
- Casey Jr. Circus Train
- Dumbo the Flying Elephant
- It's a Small World
- King Arthur Carrousel
- Mad Tea Party
- Matterhorn Bobsleds
- Mr. Toad's Wild Ride
- Peter Pan's Flight
- Pinocchio's Daring Journey
- Sleeping Beauty
  Castle Walkthrough
- Snow White Grotto
- Snow White's Scary
  Adventures
- Storybook Land Canal Boats

TOMORROWLAND
- Astro Orbitor
- Autopia
- Buzz Lightyear Astro Blasters
- Disneyland Monorail
- Disneyland Railroad
- Finding Nemo
  Submarine Voyage
- Space Mountain
- Star Tours–The Adventures Continue
- Star Wars Launch Bay
- Super Hero HQ

ADVENTURELAND
- Enchanted Tiki Room
- Indiana Jones Adventure
- Jungle Cruise
- Tarzan's Treehouse

CRITTER COUNTRY
- Davy Crockett's
  Explorer Canoes
- The Many Adventures
  of Winnie the Pooh
- Splash Mountain

ATTRACTIONS WITH HEIGHT REQUIREMENTS

- 32" or taller   Autopia (passenger)
- 54" or taller   Autopia (driver)
- 35" or taller   Gadget's Go Coaster
- 40" or taller   Big Thunder Mtn. Railroad
  Space Mountain
  Splash Mountain
  Star Tours—The
     Adventures Continue
- 42" or taller   Matterhorn Bobsleds
- 46" or taller   Indiana Jones Adventure

For safety reasons, you have to be a certain height or taller to ride some attractions.

ATTRACTIONS WITH SINGLE RIDER LINES

- Indiana Jones Adventure
- Matterhorn Bobsleds
- Splash Mountain

When Cast Members need someone to fill an empty spot on a ride, they pull people from the Single Rider line. The Single Rider line usually moves faster than the regular line but you usually are separated from others in your group.

ATTRACTIONS WITH VIDEO VERSIONS

- Finding Nemo Submarine Voyage
- Sleeping Beauty
  Castle Walkthrough

If you can't or don't want to climb stairs, there are nearby spots to view these attractions on a TV instead.

ATTRACTIONS WITH FASTPASS

- Autopia
- Big Thunder Mountain Railroad
- Buzz Lightyear Astro Blasters
- Fantasmic!
- Haunted Mansion
- Indiana Jones Adventure
- Roger Rabbit's Car Toon Spin
- Royal Theatre
- Space Mountain
- Splash Mountain
- Star Tours—The Adventures
  Continue

Free FastPass tickets can usually help you avoid crowds and long lines.

Faster Fun With FastPass

Here's how it works...

#1   Look for **FastPass machines** near the attraction.

#2   Check the **return time range** and, if it looks good to you, stick your **admission ticket** into a FastPass machine. Keep in mind, everyone in your group needs to have their **own** FastPass.

#3   The machine will give you a **printed FastPass** with your return time printed on it. Be sure to get your admission ticket back too.

#4   Come back to the attraction during your return time and go in the **special FastPass line.**

Choose wisely. Attractions run out of FastPasses as the day goes on and, when you get a FastPass, you can't get another one right away. Take a look at the **bottom** of your FastPass to see what time you can get another one.

My favorite Disney story is:

––––––––––––

The best Disney character is:

––––––––––––

The meanest Disney villian is:

––––––––––––

FUN FACT

Disney characters can sometimes be found hiding in other movies! See if you can spot Sebastian the Crab in "Aladdin," Pinocchio in "Tangled" or Rapunzel & Flynn Rider in "Frozen."

AWESOME!

★ Characters Galore

Many attractions in Disneyland are based on Disney movies. Some movies are based on classic stories, like *Cinderella*, and others are newer, like *Toy Story*. Popular characters from these movies are not only seen in attractions but can also be found strolling around the park, in shows, in parades and at official Meet n' Greets. In the shops, Disney characters are found on all sorts of souvenirs like toys, mugs and shirts. You'll see character names used for menu items and ride vehicles too. If you'd like to get to know these characters before your visit to the park, stop by your local library to brush up on your Disney tales!

HOT TIP For super, **super-short versions** of some stories, turn to page 175.

say WHat?

Guess **which** character said **what**. Draw a **speech bubble** from their name to the quote. The first one's been done for you. *Answers on page 181.*

He's no monster, Gaston— you are!

The human world...it's a mess!

Some people are worth melting for.

Do you trust me?

Frying pans. Who knew, right?

　　Aladdin　　Belle　　Flynn Rider　　Olaf　　Sebastian the Crab

Meet n' Greets at a Glance

FANTASYLAND

- Disney Princesses
- Tinker Bell and Fairy Friends

MICKEY'S TOONTOWN

- Mickey Mouse

TOMORROWLAND

- Spider-Man
- Thor
- Star Wars Characters

CRITTER COUNTRY

- Winnie the Pooh & Friends

Character Encounters

In addition to the official Meet n' Greet locations listed above, characters can be found in **various spots** all over the park. If you see a character greeting fans, check to see if there's a line. Once it's your turn you can have a short chat, take pictures and get their autograph *(see page 170)*. Characters will sign their name with a pen or use a special stamp. Some characters are around more during **special times of the year** like villains and characters from *The Nightmare Before Christmas* during the Halloween season and characters from *The Princess and the Frog* during Mardi Gras. Want to see as **many** Disney characters as possible? They are often found in these spots:

MAIN STREET USA
- Main Entrance
- Town Square
- Central Plaza

FANTASYLAND
- Snow White Grotto

MICKEY'S TOONTOWN
- Minnie's House

ADVENTURELAND
- Aladdin's Oasis

  If you see a character walking **quickly,** this usually means they're on their way somewhere and don't have time to stop.

FOOD & DRINKS at a GLANCE

◆ = Open for breakfast
● = Filtered water refill station
■ = Free soda refills/to-go cups

FULL SERVICE *Sit-down meal with waiters*	QUICK SERVICE *Order then take food to a table*	ON THE GO *Limited or no seating*
MAIN STREET USA		
• Carnation Café ◆	• Gibson Girl Ice Cream Parlor • Jolly Holiday Bakery Café ◆ • Plaza Inn ◆ ■ • Refreshment Corner	• Little Red Wagon • Market House ◆
FANTASYLAND	• Village Haus Restaurant	• Edelweiss Snacks • Troubadour Tavern ◆
MICKEY'S TOONTOWN	• Clarabelle's • Daisy's Diner • Pluto's Dog House	
TOMORROWLAND	• Redd Rockett's Pizza Port ■ • Tomorrowland Terrace ◆ ●	
ADVENTURELAND	• Bengal Barbecue	• Tiki Juice Bar
• Aladdin's Oasis		

FRONTIERLAND	• The Golden Horseshoe
	• Rancho del Zocalo
	  Restaurante ● ■
	• River Belle Terrace ◆
		• Stage Door
		  Café

NEW ORLEANS SQUARE	• French Market Restaurant ● • Royal Street Veranda	• Mint Julep Bar
• Blue Bayou Restaurant • Café Orleans		
CRITTER COUNTRY	• Harbour Galley • Hungry Bear Restaurant	

➡ There are also lots of snack carts and food stands
➡ Many restaurants have crowd-pleasing kids' menus
➡ If you have allergies or dietary restrictions, be sure to ask about all your choices as they may not be listed on the menu

★ Top 7 Sweet Treats

Some people can't visit Disneyland without having a churro. Other people have to have a Mint Julep. Which of these yummy treats sounds good to you?

#1 Mint Julep

People either love or hate this icy, non-alcoholic drink made with lime juice, lemonade, mint and sugar.
LOCATIONS: Blue Bayou Restaurant, Café Orleans, French Market Restaurant

#2 Matterhorn Macaroon

A coconut macaroon cookie is usually round but Disneyland takes this treat to new heights by forming it into the pointed peaked shape of the Matterhorn mountain and topping it with white chocolate "snow."
LOCATION: Jolly Holiday Bakery Café

#3 Candy Cane

These handmade candy canes are only made during the holiday season and are SO popular that people wait in line to get a special ticket to buy them.
LOCATION: Candy Palace

#4 Tigger Tail

Not to be confused with the yummy Tiger Tails breadsticks from Bengal Barbecue, this treat has marshmallows coated in caramel and covered in tiger-striped chocolate.
LOCATION: Pooh Corner

#5 Mickey Beignet

Pronounced "ben-yey," this pastry covered in powdered sugar is not only yummy—it's Mickey-shaped!
LOCATIONS: Café Orleans, Mint Julep Bar

 HOT TIP The **Mint Julep Bar** beignets come in a bag while **Café Orleans** serves them with dipping sauce.

#6 Churro

This sweet, crunchy treat is made from dough that's pulled through a star-shaped mold, deep fried, and sprinkled with cinnamon and sugar.
LOCATION: Various churro carts

#7 Dole Whip

There aren't many places in the world to get this pineapple soft-serve ice cream-style dessert, but Disneyland is one of them.
LOCATION: Tiki Juice Bar

SHOPS at a GLance

MAIN STREET USA

- Candy Palace
- Castle Bros.
- Chester Drawer's
- China Closet
- Crystal Arts
- Disneyana
- Disney Clothiers, Ltd.
- Disney Showcase
- Emporium
- Fortuosity Shop
- The Mad Hatter
- Main Street Magic Shop
- Main Street Photo Supply Co.
- New Century Jewelry
- Penny Arcade
- Silhouette Studio
- Storybook Store
- 20th Century Music Company

FANTASYLAND

- Bibbidi Bobbidi Boutique
- Castle Heraldry Shoppe
- Enchanted Chamber
- Fairy Tale Treasures
- It's a Small World Toy Shop
- The Mad Hatter

MICKEY'S TOONTOWN

- Gag Factory - Toontown Five & Dime

TOMORROWLAND

- Little Green Men Store Command
- Spaceport Document Control
- The Star Trader
- TomorrowLanding

ADVENTURELAND

- Adventureland Bazaar
- Indiana Jones Adventure Outpost
- South Seas Traders

FRONTIERLAND

- Bonanza Outfitters
- Leather Shop
- Pioneer Mercantile
- Westward Ho Trading Co.

NEW ORLEANS SQUARE

- Le Bat en Rouge
- Cristal d'Orleans
- La Mascarade d'Orleans
- Mlle. Antoinette's Parfumerie
- Parasol Cart
- Pieces of Eight
- Port Royal

CRITTER COUNTRY

- The Briar Patch
- Pooh Corner
- Professor Barnaby Owl's Photographic Art Studio

 Real magicians work in **Main Street Magic Shop!** Say the magic word ("please") and they'll be happy to show you some of their amazing tricks.

Do YOU collect Disney pins? ☐ Yes ☐ No
If yes, which one is your favorite?
_____

PIN TRADING

Collectible metal pins can be bought all over Disneyland and traded with Cast Members and other Guests. There are over **60,000** different pin designs featuring Disney characters, movies, attractions, events and landmarks. Many pin traders put their pins on lanyards around their neck but you can stick them on a hat, bag or anywhere you like. Look for Cast Members wearing a **dark blue** pin trading lanyard. You may also see Cast Members holding **pin boards** in front of shops where pins are sold like **Westard Ho Trading Co.** If you see a pin you want to trade for, just ask nicely. As long as you're not offering them a pin they already have, they will agree to your trade. Kids aged **3-12** can trade special **kids only** pins with Cast Members wearing **aqua blue** lanyards. Keep in mind, if you're asking to trade pins with another Guest, it's up to them whether they want to accept a trade or not, just like it's up to **YOU** when you're trading **YOUR** pins.

SAY "CHEESE!"

When you're in Disneyland, you may notice Cast Members in tan vests with really nice cameras. These folks are **Disney PhotoPass photographers.** For a fee, you can buy prints of the pictures they take of you and your group from **Main Street Photo Supply Co.** or from the **Disneyland website.** If you're interested, the first photographer you meet will give you a **PhotoPass card** with your account number. Each time you have your picture taken, give your card to the photographer. You can also ask the photographers to set up a **Magic Shot** pose where Disney characters are added to the image after it's been taken. They are also happy to take photos of you with your own camera!

★ Top 9 Shops

SO YOU KNOW...
souvenir = an item bought as a reminder of a place you've visited

These shops are so cute n' cool, they're worth exploring whether you're in the market for a **souvenir** or not!

#1 EMPORIUM

If you only have time to go in one shop in Disneyland, make it the Emporium in **Main Street USA.** It's the biggest shop in the park and has the largest selection. This shop—as well as many others in this land—has antiques and vintage touches that make you feel like you've traveled back in time.

#2 POOH CORNER

Fans of Winnie the Pooh will not want to miss this absolutely adorable spot in **Critter Country** that's part shop, part bakery, part candy store. The charming decor includes flying Heffabees, beehive-shaped lights and lots and lots of honey pots.

#3 GAG FACTORY-TOONTOWN FIVE $ DIME

Check out the funny Gag-O-Matic machine with gloved, cartoon hands moving silly props and gags like whoopee cushions, banana peels and mouse traps around the only shop in **Mickey's Toontown.**

#4 CANDY PALACE

I smell chocolate!

If you think you smell candy when you walk by this **Main Street USA** shop, you're probably right. Look under each window and you'll see a Smellitzer. These round vents pump the smell of the candy out to the streeet and tempt you to enter. Once inside, the sweetness continues with candy-colored stained glass, chandeliers dripping with crystals and sweet treats as far as the eye can see!

EXIT

SPY Look for this **cute sign** at Candy Palace. Wait—why would anyone want to **EXIT** a candy store?!

#5 MLLe. antoinette's Parfumerie

Named after 18th-century French Queen Marie Antoinette, this **New Orleans Square** shop's walls were handpainted in the 1960s by Imagineer Glendra Von Kessel. She used a technique called reverse painting where you paint on the back of a sheet of glass which is then turned into a mirror.

#6 adventureland bazaar

You'll feel like a daring explorer scouting for supplies for your next expedition when you stroll through this crowded marketplace in **Adventureland.** The sandstone walls, tiki-style grass roofs, and rustic structures create the feeling of an exotic outdoor street bazaar.

#7 The Star Trader

This futuristic *Star Wars*-themed shop in **Tomorrowland** has a ginormous X-wing starfighter, outerspace murals and cool, UFO-shaped lights.

#8 Pioneer Mercantile

Saunter back to the days of the Wild West when you enter this rustic trading post in **Frontierland.** The rough stone walls, weathered wood, animal skins and Native American decor make the perfect setting for the Western wares.

#9 The Mad Hatter

Many shops in the park sell hats but the **Fantasyland** location of The Mad Hatter might just be the best place to shop for one. Not only do they have a huge selection but the shop is totally charming with a timbered ceiling, rabbit-themed displays and chandeliers covered in carrots.

 SPY
There's something special about the **mirror** behind the counter at **The Mad Hatter.** Don't notice anything right away? Keep watching for a **smiling surprise.**

Hop aboard the Disneyland Railroad to take the Grand Circle Tour all the way around the park.

Main Street USA

What Will You Find in This Land?

ENTERTAINMENT
- Dapper Dans
- Disneyland Band
- The Hook & Ladder Co.
- Main Street Piano Player
- Pearly Band
- The Straw Hatters

ATTRACTIONS
- Disney Gallery
- Disneyland Railroad
- Fire Station
- Great Moments with
  Mr. Lincoln
- Main Street Cinema
- Main Street Vehicles

FOOD & DRINKS
- Carnation Café
- Gibson Girl Ice Cream Parlor
- Jolly Holiday Bakery Café
- Little Red Wagon
- Market House
- Plaza Inn
- Refreshment Corner

SHOPS
- Candy Palace
- Castle Bros.
- Chester Drawer's
- China Closet
- Crystal Arts
- Disneyana
- Disney Clothiers, Ltd.
- Disney Showcase
- Emporium
- Fortuosity Shop
- The Mad Hatter
- Main Street Magic Shop
- Main Street Photo Supply Co.
- New Century Jewelry
- Penny Arcade
- Silhouette Studio
- Storybook Store
- 20th Century
  Music Company

ALSO IN THIS CHAPTER
- Fun in Town Square
- Where's Mickey?
- Helpful Spots in Main Street USA
- Awesome Audio-Animatronics
- Pick Your Wheels!
- Imagineer Close-up: Mary Blair
- Be a Movie Critic!
- Old-Fashioned Fun
- Palm Reading in Disneyland?
- Unique Souvenirs
- Main Street Window Honors
- Who Shops Where?

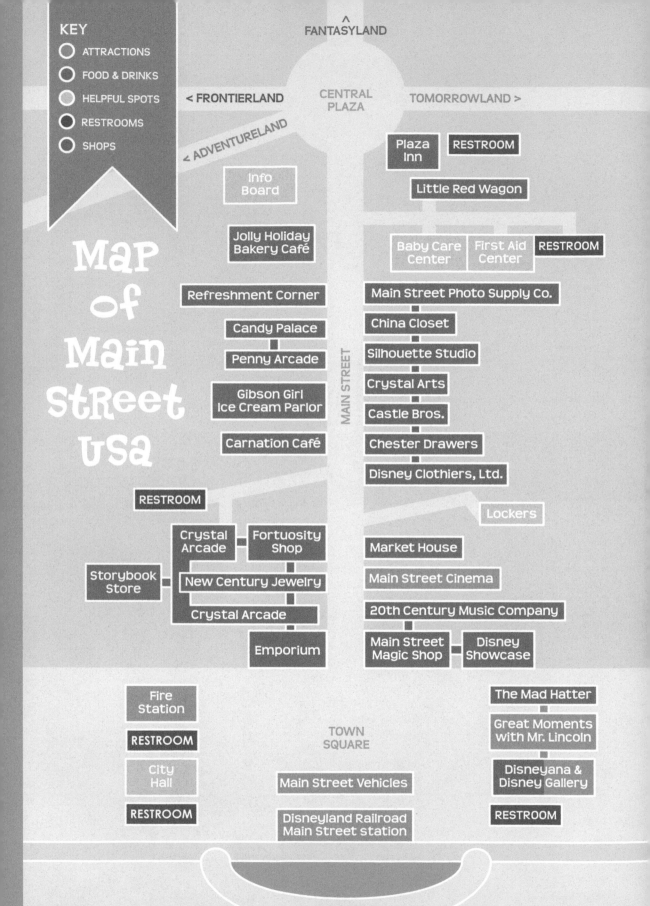

KEY

- ○ ATTRACTIONS
- ○ FOOD & DRINKS
- ○ HELPFUL SPOTS
- ● RESTROOMS
- ○ SHOPS

^
FANTASYLAND

< FRONTIERLAND

CENTRAL PLAZA

TOMORROWLAND >

< ADVENTURELAND

Map of Main Street USA

Info Board

Plaza Inn

RESTROOM

Little Red Wagon

Jolly Holiday Bakery Café

Baby Care Center

First Aid Center

RESTROOM

Main Street Photo Supply Co.

Refreshment Corner

China Closet

Candy Palace

Silhouette Studio

Penny Arcade

Crystal Arts

Gibson Girl Ice Cream Parlor

Castle Bros.

Chester Drawers

Carnation Café

Disney Clothiers, Ltd.

MAIN STREET

RESTROOM

Lockers

Crystal Arcade

Fortuosity Shop

Market House

Storybook Store

New Century Jewelry

Main Street Cinema

Crystal Arcade

20th Century Music Company

Emporium

Main Street Magic Shop

Disney Showcase

Fire Station

The Mad Hatter

RESTROOM

TOWN SQUARE

Great Moments with Mr. Lincoln

City Hall

Disneyana & Disney Gallery

Main Street Vehicles

RESTROOM

Disneyland Railroad Main Street station

RESTROOM

ENTRANCE

Step Back in Time

When you are spending the day in Disneyland, you will have a LOT of decisions to make—what ride should I go on next...do I need a rest...should I eat a giant pickle? But the first decision you have to make after you walk through the Main Entrance is "Do I go left or right?!" The good news is, no matter which way you go, you'll end up in the same place—Town Square in Main Street USA. From Town Square you can either amble down Main Street, hop aboard an old-timey vehicle or take a ride on the Disneyland Railroad. Main Street USA is made to look like an American town around the years of 1890-1910 and is one of the most charming parts of Disneyland!

★ Entertainment

For showtimes, pick up an Entertainment Times Guide at the Main Entrance, get info at City Hall or ask a friendly Cast Member.

- **Dapper Dans**—strolling barbershop quartet singers
- **Disneyland Band**—strolling marching band
- **The Hook & Ladder Co.**—vintage classics performed in front of the Fire Station
- **Main Street Piano Player**—ragtime pianist at Refreshment Corner
- **Pearly Band**—strolling, British-themed band like the one in *Mary Poppins*
- **The Straw Hatters**—strolling Dixieland jazz band

★ Fun in Town Square

City Hall

This stately building is home to Guest Relations. This is the place to go for info on anything. If you're celebrating a special occasion like a birthday or your first visit, pop in for a free button!

 Check out the **Lost Parents** sign by City Hall with **Mr. and Mrs. Darling** from *Peter Pan*.

Fire Station

Pop in for a look around this handsome fire station with horse stables, a fire pole and an antique-style fire engine. And guess what? It's okay to climb on it!

 Walt Disney had an **apartment** over the Fire Station. Look at the **upstairs window** and you may see a light on in his honor.

WHERE'S MICKEY?

A **Hidden Mickey** is where the shape of Mickey Mouse is **hidden** in Disney attractions and other spots in the park. Hidden Mickeys are used as decorations on products for sale too. Sometimes Mickey's whole body is shown but usually it's the simple **three-circle symbol** that looks like Mickey's head.

 This cabinet in City Hall has a **sideways** Hidden Mickey. Can you find it?

Little Walt Disney at the Baby Care Center!

DiSney GaLLeRY

This beautiful gallery shows off art created for or inspired by Disney. Check and see if a real Disney artist is sketching in the gallery when you're there!

The **Disneyana** shop in front of the gallery used to be a **real bank.** See if you can spy the **old bank vault** inside!

OPeRa HouSe

Disney artwork, models, memorabilia and photos are displayed here. This is also the place for a short movie called *Disneyland: The First 50 Magical Years,* and Great Moments with Mr. Lincoln. *More info on page 42.*

Check out the **model of Disneyland** from Opening Day on display in the **Opera House.**

HeLPfuL SPots in Main StReet uSa

BABY CARE CENTER
• High chairs • Changing tables
• Baby supplies

CENTRAL PLAZA INFO BOARD
• Attraction wait times
• Show times

CITY HALL
• Park maps in foreign languages
• Translation devices
• Accessibility info
• Tour & dining reservations

FIRST AID CENTER
• Medical assistance
• Bandages for boo-boos & ouchies

There are **hundreds** of Hidden Mickeys in Disneyland! Put a ✓ next to the ones you see.

MAIN STREET USA:
☐ On the stairs in Main Street Cinema
FANTASYLAND:
☐ In a window of the Big Ben clock in Peter Pan's Flight
MICKEY'S TOONTOWN:
☐ On the hubcaps on the wheels of Mickey's car
FRONTIERLAND:
☐ On a vent in front of the stage in The Golden Horseshoe
CRITTER COUNTRY:
☐ On the shelf over a sales counter in Pooh Corner

Want to search for even more Mickeys? The website **www.FindingMickey.com** lists lots more to find. HAPPY HUNTING...

FUN FACT

Abraham Lincoln had NO middle name & liked to be called "Lincoln" not "Abe."

AH HA!

★ Great Moments with Mr. Lincoln

Would you like to see an Abraham Lincoln robot talking and moving? Then you won't want to miss this show at the Opera House. This attraction was first shown in 1964 at the New York World's Fair where it was a huge hit. A year later, it was moved to Disneyland. After a short movie about Lincoln and America's Civil War, the curtains part to show the Lincoln Audio-Animatronic figure seated on stage. You might feel like he looks so real he could stand up—and then he will!

INDOOR SHOW ★ est. 1965 ★ calm & mellow

HOT TIP

WATCH OUT! This attraction is pretty **educational.** If you're not careful, you just might learn something.

AWESOME AUDIO-ANIMATRONICS

Walt Disney was fascinated by **mechanical toy animals** he had bought on a trip to Europe. But he wondered if it was possible to make something even **better.** The Disney Imagineers set to work and called their creations **Audio-Animatronics,** a combo of:

audio = sound
anima = animated or moving
tronics = electronics

In addition to the Abraham Lincoln Audio-Animatronic, Imagineers have created **many more** for many more attractions. Today, you can find Audio-Animatronics all over Disneyland like **pirates** in Pirates of the Caribbean, **birds** in Enchanted Tiki Room, **ghosts** in Haunted Mansion, **abominable creatures** on Matterhorn Bobsleds, **woodland animals** on Splash Mountain and many, many more!

★ Main Street Vehicles

et ready to ride in style! Main Street USA's vintage-style vehicles will take you on a one-way trip up or down Main Street going from Town Square to Central Plaza in front of Sleeping Beauty Castle.

OLD-FASHIONED VEHICLES ★ CALM & MELLOW ★
est. 1955

HOT TIP If you want to ride in a Main Street Vehicle, **keep in mind** they stop running before dark and won't be out when the park is crowded!

PICK YOUR WHEELS!

If you could take **one** of these home, which one would you pick? Put a ✔ next to your choice.

☐ **Fire Engine:**
1910s-style
Fire Truck

☐ **Omnibus:**
1920s-style
Double-Decker Bus

☐ **Jitney/Horseless Carriage:**
1900s-style Car

☐ **Horse-Drawn Streetcars:**
1800s-style Horse-Powered Trolleys

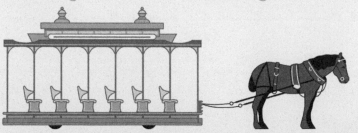

FUN FACT

The cannons around the flag pole in Town Square are authentic French weapons from the 19th century.

OOH LA LA!

CENTRAL PLAZA

MAIN STREET

TOWN SQUARE

ENTRANCE

43

FUN FACT

The Lilly Belle train car was named after Walt's wife Lillian, who helped design the interior. This elegant, Victorian-style parlor car with velvet furniture & lace curtains is sometimes used as a caboose.

LUXE!

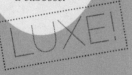

MICKEY'S TOONTOWN

NEW ORLEANS SQUARE

TOMORROWLAND

MAIN STREET USA

"The only way to be sure of catching a train is to miss the one before it."
—G. K. CHESTERSON

★ Disneyland Railroad

Sit back and enjoy unique views of the park aboard a vintage steam train. The trains usually come about every ten minutes and four stations circle the park. Hop on for a stop or two, or take the Grand Circle Tour to end up back where you started. There are four engines named after real-life locomotive legends—Fred Gurley, C.K. Holliday, Ernest S. Marsh and E.P. Ripley—and one named after animator and train enthusiast Ward Kimball. If you love trains as much as Walt Disney did, pop into the Main Street Station to enjoy artifacts and displays including an exhibit about the train Walt had in his own backyard!

HOT TIP Check in at the **Main Street station** first thing in the a.m. to try for a spot on the **tender seat** next to the conductor or a ride in the **Lilly Belle** train car.

steam-train ride
—est.—
1955
★ calm & mellow ★

DISNEYLAND

TIME MACHINE

1953	1955	1958	1966
Concept drawings for Disneyland by Imagineer Herb Ryman show a train circling the park.	*Walt Disney drives one of the two Disneyland Railroad trains on Opening Day. All aboard!*	*The Grand Canyon Diorama is added as a sight to see between the Tomorrowland & Main Street stations.*	*The Primeval World Diorama, first seen at the 1964 New York World's Fair, is added next to the Grand Canyon Diorama.*

IMAGINEER CLOSE-UP: MARY BLAIR

Mary Blair trained as a traditional artist but came up with a happy, childlike, **mega-colorful** artistic style all her own. In 1940, she began working as a **Disney animator.** She painted beautiful **color** and **style designs** that helped create the **look and feel** of movies like *Cinderella, Alice In Wonderland* and *Peter Pan.* Mary's unique style had a **BIG** impact on Walt Disney who was a huge fan of her work. She had left the Disney Company when he asked her to help with the **It's a Small World** attraction. Later, she created two giant, outdoor tile **murals** where Star Tours and Buzz Lightyear Astro Blasters are today. If you visit **Disney's Contemporary Resort** in Florida, be sure to check out Mary's incredible **90-foot tall** mural in the lobby!

FROM TOP TO BOTTOM:
- "The Bandstand" by Mary Blair
- Mary sketching in her studio
- The crazily colorful crocodile in It's a Small World

RATE THIS ATTRACTION

- Never. Again.
- Not so hot.
- Pretty cool...
- Way cool!
- Awesome!!
- AHH, MY FAVE!!!

One word I'd use to describe this attraction:

_ _ _ _ _ _ _ _ _ _

FuN FaCT

A mannequin named Tilly sits in the ticket booth at Main Street Cinema. Take a look at her name tag & you'll see she's from the town Walt Disney lived in when he was a boy— Marceline, Missouri.

HI TILLY!

★ # Main Street Cinema

MoVie THeaTeR
— est. —
1955
CaLM & MeLLoW

ℕo tickets needed at this theater! Pop into this multi-screen theater anytime and check out six animated classics including Mickey and Minnie Mouse's *Steamboat Willie* cartoon. This is a cool place to take a break from the hustle and bustle of Main Street and spend some time with the mouse who started it all.

 HOT TIP There are no chairs inside the Main Street Cinema but the **raised platform** in the middle gives little ones a better view.

Be a MoVie CRitiC!

Main Street Cinema shows these **cartoons** over and over in a loop. Put a ✓ next to the ones you watched and color in how many stars they should get.

★ = not so good ★★ = okay ★★★ = good
★★★★ = great ★★★★★ = awesome

- Steamboat Willie ☆☆☆☆☆
- Plane Crazy ☆☆☆☆☆
- The Moose Hunt ☆☆☆☆☆
- Traffic Troubles ☆☆☆☆☆
- The Dognapper ☆☆☆☆☆
- Mickey's Polo Team ☆☆☆☆☆

OLD-FaSHioNeD FuN

Back in the old days, penny arcades had games that cost only **a penny** and some of the antique amusements in the **Penny Arcade** still do! Other machines cost a quarter or two. The sweet treats from the **Candy Palace** next door have almost taken over, but you can still have your fortune told by the mysterious gypsy **Esmeralda** or hear a cheery song played on the **Orchestrion Machine.** There are **Mutoscopes** where you put in your coins to see a short movie, a **True Grip Challenge** machine to see how strong you are and even a **Kiss-O-Meter** to "measure the thrill of your kisses." Take your pick and pop in your coins!

SPY Look on the outside of the **Penny Arcade** to spy a **giant penny.** Can you guess why it has **"1901"** on it? For a hint, turn to page 10.

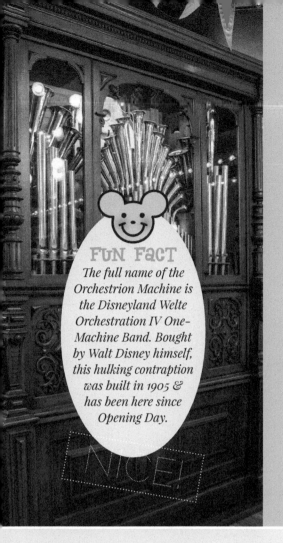

FuN FacT
The full name of the Orchestrion Machine is the Disneyland Welte Orchestration IV One-Machine Band. Bought by Walt Disney himself, this hulking contraption was built in 1905 & has been here since Opening Day.

NICE!

PaLm ReaDiNG IN DiSNeyLaND?

Across from the Penny Arcade sits a blue building with signs that say **Fargo's Palm Parlor.** What's a **palm parlor?** It's a place where a fortune teller reads the lines in the palm of your hand to tell your **fortune!** But, the signs on this building are only for **decoration** and there's not **really** a palm parlor inside. So, why is it called <u>Fargo's</u> Palm Parlor? It's in honor of legendary Imagineer **Rolly Crump** whose middle name is Fargo. Disneyland has a similar sign in Frontierland which reads **Crockett & Russel Hat Co.** in honor of **Davy Crockett** and his best friend **George Russel.** Though the sign makes the building look like a hat shop from the outside, the inside is part of a clothing shop called **Bonanza Outfitters.**

HOT TIP The front porch of Fargo's Palm Parlor is a **wonderful, quiet spot** to sit and watch the world go by!

★ Food & Drinks

MARKET HOUSE

This corner café has a few cozy spots by the potbelly stove in the Book Rest nook where you can enjoy your treats.
• *Coffee* • *Pastries* • *Smoothies*

HOT TIP Pick up an **old-fashioned phone** by the door to listen in on an 1890 party line conversation!

carnation café

With red carnation flowers on every table, this cute café serves delish dishes to enjoy inside, or outside near the charming gazebo.
• *Chicken-fried chicken* • *Meatloaf*
• *Pancakes*

GIBSON GIRL Ice CReam PaRLor

This pleasant parlor with indoor seating is named after artist Charles Dana Gibson's famous "Gibson Girl" drawings.
• *Hot fudge sundaes* • *Ice cream cones*
• *Ice cream floats*

SPY Peek in the window next to the main counter to see the **waffle cones** being made!

LittLe ReD WaGon

This walk-up wagon is home to Disneyland's famously delicious corn dogs.
• *Apples* • *Chips* • *Corn dogs*

Refreshment Corner

Time your visit right and you can enjoy live music from a talented ragtime piano player at this refreshing outdoor spot. If you're a soda fan, ask about flavors you can order that aren't on the menu.

• *Chili* • *Hot dogs* • *Pretzels*

 Alice and the Mad Hatter often stop by for a game of **Musical Chairs** at this corner café!

 Try to find the **half-red, half-white light bulb** by the entrance. This half-and-half bulb keeps the pattern of the <u>odd</u> number of red and white bulbs <u>even</u>!

Jolly Holiday Bakery Café

If you love *Mary Poppins,* you won't want to miss this cheerful outdoor café named after a song written for the movie by legendary Disney songwriters, the brothers Richard and Robert Sherman.

• *Muffins* • *Salads*
• *Sandwiches* • *Soups*

 See if you can spot any of Mary's **penguin pals** decorating this café!

Plaza Inn

Perch on the pretty porch or patio or dine inside in a setting fit for prince or princess with glittering chandeliers, glimmering brass and very, *very* fancy curtains!

• *Carrot cake* • *Fried chicken* • *Mickey waffles* • *Pot roast*

 Plaza Inn is the place for the **Minnie & Friends Character Breakfast.**

DID YOU EAT IN MAIN STREET USA?
☐ Yes ☐ No
If yes, where?

_____

What'd ya have?

_____

_____

_____

Was it good?
☐ Yes ☐ No
☐ Maybe So

 FUN FACT

Plaza Inn was designed by Walt Disney's wife Lillian. This stunning restaurant has ceilings, floors & woodwork salvaged from real old buildings. Walt loved to eat here & even had a private lounge for special guests.

FANCY!

★ Unique Souvenirs

Gypsy Fortune

Esmeralda sits in the entrance to the Penny Arcade ready to reveal all to any who cross her palm with silver. After moving her hand slowly over her mysterious playing cards, your fortune will pop out below. And if you drop another coin in the slot, she'll tell you more. This gypsy is so popular with Disneyland fans that Disney has even made collectible Esmeralda Vinylmation toys and pins!

 Some of the **cards** in front of Esmeralda have images from **Haunted Mansion** on them.

SO YOU KNOW...
SILHOUETTE = a solid black shape made from the outline of an object

Paper Silhouette

Amazingly skilled paper artists cut your **silhouette** freehand in about 60 seconds while you watch at Silhouette Studio!

Your Favorite Art

The Art on Demand machine inside Disneyana lets you pick which Disney picture you want from hundreds of choices!

Main Street Window Honors

The signs on the windows in Main Street USA honor **real people** who worked for Disneyland as artists, designers, sculptors, landscapers, carpenters, writers, executives and more. The windows have the person's **name** and a made-up **job** and/or **company** related to what they did for the park **or** their hobby. But one of the windows pays tribute to someone who actually **never** worked for Disneyland at all. A second-story window of the Emporium has the name of Walt Disney's father, **Elias**. Because Elias Disney was a builder, his window says: "CONTRACTOR EST. 1895." Look around and you'll see there are many **Main Street Window Honors**. Like to know more about the stories behind them? The book *Main Street Windows* by Jeff Heimbuch tells the tale behind each and every window in each and every Disney resort!

WHO SHOPS WHERE?

Which Disney character might shop in which of these **fake stores?** Draw a line to connect the character's name with their **shopping bag.** The first one's been done for you.

Answers on page 181.

Beastly Books

ARENDELLE SNOWMAN SUPPLIES

BIG SUMMER BLOWOUT!

Belle

Cinderella

THE HUNNY POT

Genie

Minnie Mouse

The Glass Slipper

the right shoe can change your life

Rapunzel

LAMPS R-US

Pinocchio

Cruella de Vil

Bow Boutique

Olaf

Fabulous Furs

Winnie the Pooh

Ariel

Real Boy Clothing

Dinglehoppers

ODDITIES AND CURIOS FROM THE HUMAN WORLD

Kingdom of Corona Lanterns

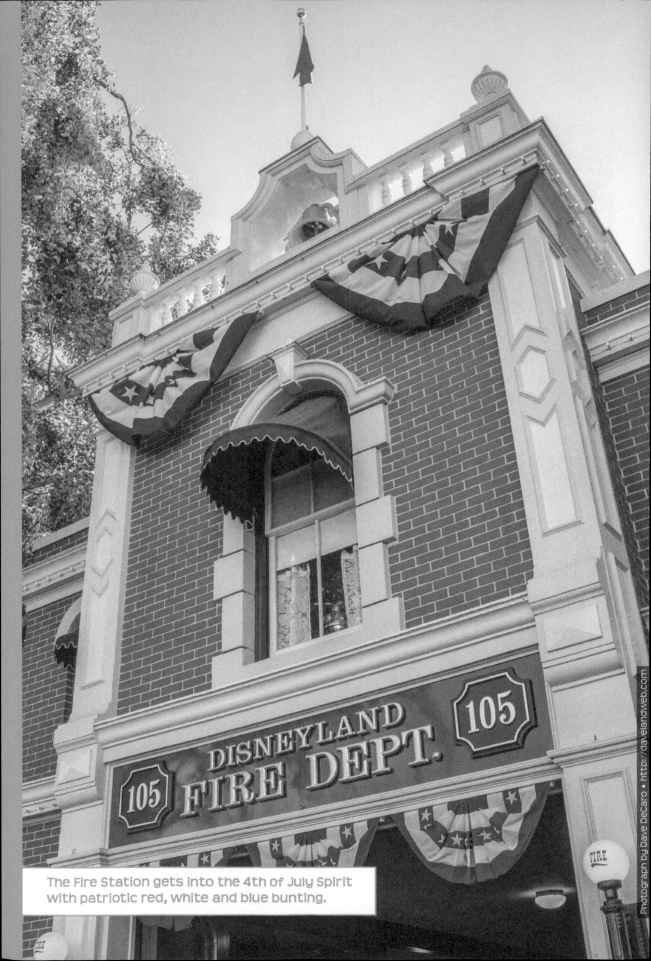

The Fire Station gets into the 4th of July Spirit with patriotic red, white and blue bunting.

DISNEYLAND FIRE DEPT.

105
105

FIRE

FantasyLand

What Will You Find in This Land?

ENTERTAINMENT
- Frozen
- Mickey and the Magical Map

ATTRACTIONS
- Alice In Wonderland
- Casey Jr. Circus Train
- Dumbo the Flying Elephant
- It's a Small World
- King Arthur Carrousel
- Mad Tea Party
- Matterhorn Bobsleds
- Mr. Toad's Wild Ride
- Peter Pan's Flight
- Pinocchio's Daring Journey
- Sleeping Beauty Castle Walkthrough
- Snow White Grotto
- Snow White's Scary Adventures
- Storybook Land Canal Boats

FOOD & DRINKS
- Edelweiss Snacks
- Troubadour Tavern
- Village Haus Restaurant

SHOPS
- Bibbidi Bobbidi Boutique
- Castle Heraldry Shoppe
- Enchanted Chamber
- Fairy Tale Treasures
- It's a Small World Toy Shop
- The Mad Hatter

MEET N' GREETS
- Disney Princesses
- Tinker Bell and Fairy Friends

ALSO IN THIS CHAPTER
- What's in a Name?
- Boat Name Scrambles!
- Imagineer Close-up: Marc & Alice Davis
- Princess Primer
- FAQs About the Mad Hatter
- Roastie-Toasties!
- Unique Souvenirs
- Guess the Coat of Arms!

MAP of FANTASYLAND

KEY
- ATTRACTIONS
- FOOD & DRINKS
- RESTROOMS
- SHOPS

Fantasyland Theatre

Troubadour Tavern

RESTROOM

It's a Small World

It's a Small World Toy Shop

< MICKEY'S TOONTOWN

REST SPOT

Casey Jr. Circus Train

Dumbo the Flying Elephant

Storybook Land Canal Boats

Edelweiss Snacks

King Arthur Carrousel

Mad Tea Party

RESTROOM

The Mad Hatter

Village Haus Restaurant

Pinocchio's Daring Journey

Mr. Toad's Wild Ride

Alice in Wonderland

Matterhorn Bobsleds

Snow White's Scary Adventures

Peter Pan's Flight

RESTROOM

Bibbidi Bobbidi Boutique

Castle Heraldry Shoppe

Enchanted Chamber

Sleeping Beauty Castle Walkthrough

Snow White Grotto

Royal Hall

FANTASY FAIRE

< FRONTIERLAND

Pixie Hollow

Fairy Tale Treasures

Royal Theatre

MAIN STREET USA >

TOMORROWLAND >

Fantastic Fun

You'll feel like you've stepped into the pages of a fairytale as you explore the cozy cottages, Tudor-style buildings and stately stone arches of Fantasyland. The cherry on the cake is Sleeping Beauty's perfectly pink castle surrounded by a moat with graceful swans and playful ducks. Fantasyland has more rides than any of the park's other lands, and is one of the most popular parts of the park. The newest section of Fantasyland is Fantasy Faire, a quaint village square nestled near Sleeping Beauty Castle that fits right in with the storybook charm of Fantasyland!

SPY Look for many **delightful details** around Fantasy Faire like a music box you crank yourself, Figaro the Cat from Pinocchio, and the letters "CPG" which honor the **Carnation Plaza Gardens** which used to be here.

★ Entertainment

For showtimes, pick up an Entertainment Times Guide at the Main Entrance, get info at City Hall or ask a friendly Cast Member.

- **Frozen**—live musical stage show at the Royal Theatre
- **Mickey and the Magical Map**—live musical stage show at Fantasyland Theatre

FUN FACT

Sleeping Beauty has three names: her real name (Aurora), her name when she's in hiding (Briar Rose) & her nickname (Sleeping Beauty).

WHEW!

"I must say, I really felt quite distressed at not receiving an invitation."
—MALEFICENT

★ Sleeping Beauty Castle Walkthrough

INDOOR WALK-THROUGH • EST. 1957 • LIVELY & exciting

Sleeping Beauty's majestic castle was inspired by a real castle in Germany called Neuschwanstein. When new visitors come to Disneyland and see the castle, grown-ups usually say, "It's smaller than I thought it would be!" and kids usually say, "Can I go inside?" The answer to that is... YES! As you climb the stairs and wind through dark, narrow passageways, you'll see displays inspired by artist Eyvind Earle's incredible paintings for the original movie that tell the timeless tale of Sleeping Beauty.

HOT TIP Take your time in the **Corridor of Goons** inside the castle to see some **special surprises!**

HELLO my name is
Princess Aurora

HELLO my name is
Briar Rose

HELLO my name is
Sleeping Beauty

TIME MACHINE

1697
"The Beauty Sleeping in the Wood" by Charles Perrault is published.

1955
Disneyland opens with the castle front & center but no one's allowed inside until 1957.

1959
Disney's animated movie "Sleeping Beauty" hits theaters. Sweet dreams!

2014
A live-action version of the Sleeping Beauty story called "Maleficent" hits theaters.

FUN FACTS ABOUT THE CASTLE

The castle gets dressed up for special occasions! To celebrate Disneyland's 60th Anniversary, it was draped in blue banners & covered in diamond-like jewels.

There are little-known passages through the castle to Tomorrowland & Frontierland.

Many people think the crest over the entrance to the castle is the Disney family crest. Not so! It's actually the crest of Richard the Lionheart.

The castle's drain spouts are shaped like Sleeping Beauty's squirrel friends.

There's a **time capsule** shaped like the castle in the front courtyard. It'll be opened in 2035, forty years after it was buried. Save the date!

The drawbridge really does raise & lower but it's used very rarely. Guests saw it in action on Opening Day in 1955 & again when Fantasyland was revamped in 1983.

The spires are painted with real 22-karat gold paint!

I think I'll make the castle green...

Make it blue!

No, no, no! It's perfect as it is.

SO YOU KNOW...
time capsule = container that's filled with items from the current times to be buried and opened in the future.

★ Snow White Grotto

est. **1961** — OUTDOOR area · calm & mellow

In this peaceful spot near Sleeping Beauty Castle, you will find a *lovely* waterfall with statues of Snow White, the *seven dwarfs* and adorable woodland creatures. There is also a *wishing well* where you can toss in a coin and make a wish. Listen carefully and you can hear Snow White singing about *her* wish!

HOT TIP Disney characters often hang around in **the grotto area** visiting with Guests.

SPY A **sign** on the wishing well says: "Your wishes will help children everywhere." Coins thrown in the well are donated to **children's charities.**

RATE THIS ATTRACTION
- ☐ Never. Again.
- ☐ Not so hot.
- ☐ Pretty cool...
- ☐ Way cool!
- ☐ Awesome!!
- ☐ AHH, MY FAVE!!!

One word I'd use to describe this attraction:

_ _ _ _ _ _ _ _ _ _ _ _

FUN FACT
Walt Disney was given the statues in Snow White Grotto as a gift but he wasn't sure they would look right. The Snow White statue was the same height as the dwarfs! To make it seem taller, it was placed near the top of the waterfall.

SMART!

"...anyone could see that the prince was charming, the only one for me."
—SNOW WHITE

TIME MACHINE

1812	1937	1955	1961
"Snow White" by the Brothers Grimm is published in Germany. Wunderbar!	*"Snow White & the Seven Dwarfs" hits theaters.*	*Snow White's Scary Adventures is an Opening Day attraction in Disneyland.*	*Make a wish! Snow White Grotto opens.*

Snow White's Scary Adventures

Hop into a ride car that looks a lot like the dwarfs' cozy beds—each with one of their names on the front. It's off to an adventure you'll go as you zip through the dwarfs' cottage, the jewel mine where they work, the Queen's chamber and an eerie forest. Is this ride "scary?" Well, it is dark and spooky, and the Evil Queen is in there, both as herself and in her Old Hag disguise. If you do feel scared, close your eyes and remember that in two minutes it will all be over!

HOT TIP Touch the **golden apple** near the entrance to this ride for a **surprise!**

SPY Look at the **large window** over the entrance. Are the curtains closed? If so, keep watching...**if you dare!**

INDOOR DARK RIDE ★ est. 1955 ★ lively & exciting

FUN FACT

At first, Snow White wasn't in her own ride! The idea was that the rider was seeing the scenes from Snow White's point of view. After years of people saying "But where was Snow White?" Imagineers decided to add her to the ride.

GOOD IDEA!

What's in a Name?

When **naming** the dwarfs, the Disney team thought of the **ideas** below. Put a ✓ next to the **seven** names they chose! *Answers on page 181.*

- [ ] Bashful
- [ ] Burpy
- [ ] Dirty
- [ ] Doc
- [ ] Dopey
- [ ] Grumpy
- [ ] Happy
- [ ] Hungry
- [ ] Jumpy
- [ ] Puffy
- [ ] Sleepy
- [ ] Sneezy

Aw, shucks...

How ya feeling?

YAWN!!

Hmph!

I just can't stop smiling!

Ahh-CHOO!

I don't know if I can talk, I never tried.

FUN FACT

Everyone's favorite snowman sits on a building near Pinocchio's Daring Journey because there used to be "Frozen" Meet n' Greets there.

OLAF!

★ Pinocchio's Daring Journey

MAY BE SCARY ⚠

INDOOR DARK RIDE ★ LIVELY & EXCITING ★
-EST.- **1983**

Board a woodcarver's cart and go on an adventure with the puppet Pinocchio! You'll see evil Stromboli and his puppet theatre, decadent Pleasure Island where naughty boys are turned into donkeys, and that mean Monstro the Whale. There are friendly faces too, like Cleo the Goldfish, Figaro the Cat and Jiminy Cricket. In the end, Pinocchio makes it home to Geppetto where the Blue Fairy turns him into a real boy at last!

Photograph by Dave DeCaro • http://davelandweb.com

TIME MACHINE

1881
Italian writer Carlo Collodi writes "The Adventures of Pinocchio."

1940
Disney's animated movie "Pinocchio" hits theaters.

1955
Disneyland opens with Canal Boats of the World—later renamed Storybook Land Canal Boats.

1983
Hey diddly dee! Fantasyland has a major overhaul & reopens with the brand new Pinocchio's Daring Journey.

Storybook Land Canal Boats

Outdoor Boat Ride · *Calm & Mellow* · EST. 1955

Sail right into Monstro the Whale's mouth to enter the amazing *miniature* world of Storybook Land! Your tour guide will tell you all about the many *wonders* you're passing, as you sit in a brightly painted European-style *canal boat* named after a Disney character. As the boat gently cruises through the winding *waterways*, you'll see tiny homes and villages from beloved Disney movies like *Aladdin*, *Cinderella* and *Frozen*.

SPY Check it out—Monstro the Whale's eyes **open and close,** and steam comes out of his **blowhole!**

FUN FACT
The red & white lighthouse near the entrance to this ride used to be a ticket booth when there were separate tickets for rides.

OH!

Boat Name SCRAMBLES!

Using the **helpful hints** below, unscramble the names of the **Storybook Land Canal Boats.** The first one's been done for you. *Answers on page 181.*

Scramble	Hint	Scramble	Hint
LFANEI — *Faline*	Bambi's sweet deer girlfriend	AARRUO	No spinning wheels for her
DNWEY	She's a Darling friend to Peter	AKRNTIA	She lives in Sleepy Hollow
SYIDA	Lady duck who's sweet on Donald	NSOW HEWIT	Princess with seven friends
ELAIC	She fell down a rabbit hole	KTIREN LELB	Peter Pan's petite pixie pal
ADELECNIRL	She went to the ball in style	IRALE	Also known as The Little Mermaid
LELEB	This beauty loves a beast	LFORA, AFUNA & RMERYEAWERHT	
WREFOL	Bambi's pal—or, what's in a garden	The three good fairies from *Sleeping Beauty*	

RATE THIS ATTRACTION

- ☐ Never. Again.
- ☐ Not so hot.
- ☐ Pretty cool...
- ☐ Way cool!
- ☐ Awesome!!
- ☐ AHH, MY FAVE!!!

One word I'd use
to describe this
attraction:

_____

FUN FACT

Peter Pan's Flight is filled with fiber optic lights. These teensy-tiny lights shine through teensy-tiny clear tubes & make a very magical glow.

BRILLIANT!

"Now, think of the happiest things. It's the same as having wings."
—PETER PAN

★ Peter Pan's Flight

INDOOR DARK RIDE ✶ *est.* **1955** ✶ *lively & exciting*

You can fly, you can fly, you can fly! Well, your pirate ship can fly—it's been sprinkled with pixie dust. All you have to do is think happy thoughts and you're off on a magical flight through the Darling's nursery and over the rooftops of London to the island of Never Land—a magical place where children never have to grow up. After Peter Pan battles Captain Hook, Peter and the Darling children set sail for London but Hook won't be so lucky!

SPY Look carefully at the **blocks in the nursery** near Nana the Dog to see if they spell anything!

TIME MACHINE

1904
J.M. Barrie writes "Peter Pan" & little Walter Disney later plays him in a school play. Awwwww!

1953
Disney's animated movie "Peter Pan" hits theaters.

1955
Peter Pan's Flight is an Opening Day attraction in Disneyland.

2008
Pixie Hollow opens featuring Peter Pan's faithful fairy friend Tinker Bell & her pixie pals.

"Don't you understand, Tink? You mean more to me than anything."
—PETER PAN

★ Meet n' Greets

Fantasyland has two official Meet n' Greets. Royal Hall in Fantasy Faire is the place to meet up to three **Disney Princesses.** You never know who'll be there —Belle, Cinderella, Mulan, Sleeping Beauty, Snow White or others. Like to meet **Tinker Bell and Fairy Friends?** Flit over to Pixie Hollow! As you walk down the path, the plants and flowers get bigger—or are you really getting smaller?! Tinker Bell herself might be there or her pals Fawn, Iridessa, Periwinkle, Rosetta, Silvermist, Terence or Vidia.

 If you're in the Pixie Hollow area after dark, check out the little **fountain show** every 15 minutes in the pond near the path!

IMAGINEER CLOSE-UP: MARC & ALICE DAVIS

Alice Estes was studying **costume design** when she met an **animation teacher** named Marc Davis. Later, when Marc was working on Disney's *Sleeping Beauty,* he called her in to help. Romance was in the air and the talented duo fell in love and got married. When Alice began working as an Imagineer, she created costumes for **It's a Small World** and then **Pirates of the Caribbean.** She joked, "I went from sweet little children to dirty old men overnight." Marc started out as an animator and designed many of Disney's most famous animated female characters like **Tinker Bell, Snow White** and **Alice.** In his career as an Imagineer, he designed Audio-Animatronic figures for **Jungle Cruise, It's a Small World, Pirates of the Caribbean, Haunted Mansion** and more. In other words, Marc **designed** the characters and Alice **dressed** them. What a team!

Princess Primer

NAME Snow White
FROM *Snow White and the Seven Dwarfs*, 1937
HOME A fairytale kingdom
QUOTE "Why, Grumpy, you do care!"
ANIMAL FRIENDS Woodland creatures
TRUE LOVE The Prince
SPECIAL TALENT Befriends woodland creatures

NAME Cinderella
FROM *Cinderella*, 1950
HOME A fairytale kingdom
QUOTE "But, you see, I have the other slipper."
ANIMAL FRIENDS Gus and Jaq the mice
TRUE LOVE Prince Charming
SPECIAL TALENT Dances the night away

NAME Aurora
FROM *Sleeping Beauty*, 1959
HOME A fairytale kingdom
QUOTE "If you dream a thing more than once, it's sure to come true."
ANIMAL FRIENDS Woodland creatures
TRUE LOVE Prince Phillip
SPECIAL TALENT Sleeps like a rock

NAME Ariel
FROM *The Little Mermaid*, 1989
HOME Under the sea
QUOTE "Daddy, I love him!"
ANIMAL FRIENDS Sebastian the Crab and Flounder the Fish
TRUE LOVE Prince Eric
SPECIAL TALENT Sings like an angelfish

NAME Belle
FROM *Beauty and the Beast*, 1991
HOME France
QUOTE "Some people use their imagination."
ANIMAL FRIEND Philippe the Horse
TRUE LOVE The Beast
SPECIAL TALENT Loves to read

NAME Jasmine
FROM *Aladdin*, 1992
HOME Agrabah
QUOTE "If I do marry, I want it to be for love."
ANIMAL FRIEND Rajah the Tiger
TRUE LOVE Aladdin
SPECIAL TALENT Travels by carpet

NAME Pocahontas
FROM *Pocahontas*, 1995
HOME Virginia, USA
QUOTE "There must be
a better way."
ANIMAL FRIENDS Meeko the
Racoon and Flit the
Hummingbird
TRUE LOVE John Smith
SPECIAL TALENT Canoes
down rapids

NAME Mulan
FROM *Mulan*, 1998
HOME China
QUOTE "Just because I look
like a man doesn't mean I
have to smell like one."
ANIMAL FRIEND Mushu
the Dragon
TRUE LOVE Li Shang
SPECIAL TALENT Practices
martial arts

NAME Tiana
FROM *The Princess and
the Frog*, 2009
HOME Louisiana, USA
QUOTE "There is no way I'm
kissing a frog and eating a
bug in the same day."
ANIMAL FRIENDS Ray the
Firefly and Louis the Alligator
TRUE LOVE Prince Naveen
SPECIAL TALENT Cooks the
best gumbo in town

NAME Rapunzel
FROM *Tangled*, 2010
HOME Corona
QUOTE "Best. Day. Ever!"
ANIMAL FRIEND Pascal
the Chameleon
TRUE LOVE Eugene
"Flynn Rider" Fitzherbert
SPECIAL TALENT Skilled
at painting

NAME Merida
FROM *Brave*, 2012
HOME Scotland
QUOTE "Our fate lives
within us."
ANIMAL FRIEND Angus
the Horse
TRUE LOVE None, but she
does love that horse.
SPECIAL TALENT Excels
in archery

NAME Anna
FROM *Frozen*, 2013
HOME Arendelle
QUOTE "It's true love!"
ANIMAL FRIEND Sven
the Reindeer
TRUE LOVE It's complicated
SPECIAL TALENT Gives
ice-thawing hugs

INDOOR DARK RIDE ★ est. 1955 ★ LIVELY & exciting

Demon illustration by Sam Carter • SamCarterArt.com

FUN FACT

On the shield over the door to Toad Hall are the Latin words "Toadi Acceleratio Semper Absurda" which means "Speeding with Toad is always absurd."

FUNNY!

★ Mr. Toad's Wild Ride

Hang on tight for a wild n' crazy ride. Toad is a maniac behind the wheel—and so are you! You'll drive your car right through his fancy house before speeding through the countryside with the police in hot pursuit. Down at the docks you'll crash into TNT-filled barrels, explode through a brick wall and more, before you're sent to see the judge for your punishment. The bad news is, you'll end up where bad people go. The good news is, it's just a ride!

HOT TIP There's an **extra ride car** in front of Mr. Toad's house that you can climb in for a **cute photo!**

SPY The ride cars are named **Mr. Toad, Ratty, Moley, MacBadger, Cyril, Winky** and **Weasel**. Look on your car to see which one you get!

TIME MACHINE

1908
"The Wind in the Willows" by Kenneith Grahame is published & features Mr. Toad.

1949
Disney's animated movie "The Adventures of Ichabod & Mr. Toad" hits theaters.

1955
Mr. Toad's Wild Ride is an Opening Day attraction in Disneyland.

1983
Mr. Toad's Wild Ride building is updated from a castle tent to a stately manor house. Nice digs!

King Arthur Carrousel

Spelled with TWO r's!

The story goes that Walt Disney thought of creating Disneyland while he sat on a bench watching his **daughters** ride a merry-go-round. Disney scouts found an amazing antique carousel in **Canada** and brought it to California to fix it up for Disneyland. Benches were removed and more horses were added. Later, panels were painted with scenes from **Sleeping Beauty**. Every horse has a name and is handcarved with unique details. Will you ride **Baby** who has a golden cherub hitching a ride on the side, gold-toothed **Doubloon** who wears a purple, blue and orange saddle, or the lead horse **Jingles** who's decked out in rows of bells and *Mary Poppins* imagery?

antique carousel · calm & mellow · EST. 1955

HOT TIP In front of the carousel sits a **sword stuck in an anvil** just like the one in the legend of King Arthur.

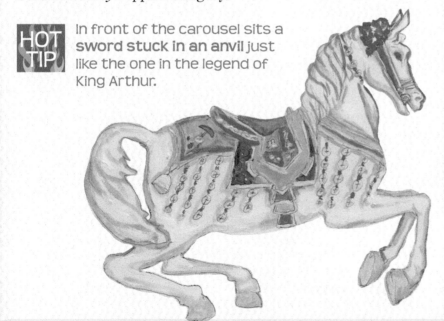

FUN FACT

There used to only be ONE white horse on King Arthur Carrousel but it was SO popular that ALL the horses were painted white in 1975.

WHOA!

"I'm in an awful pickle. I'm king!"
—KING ARTHUR

TIME MACHINE

1875	1938	1955	1963
Dentzel handcrafts the carousel in Philadelphia, Pennsylvania.	T.H. White's book "The Sword in the Stone" about King Arthur's boyhood is published.	Disneyland opens with the restored antique carousel as an Opening Day attraction.	Disney's animated movie "The Sword in the Stone" hits theaters, jumping hogtoads!

FUN FACT

The music for the Dumbo ride comes from a fancy building that houses an authentic Gavioli band organ which was made in 1915.

WOW!

Mini Quiz!

Can you guess Dumbo's real name?

Answer on page 181.

- ◻ Ears McGillicutty
- ◻ Jumbo, Jr.
- ◻ Timothy

DUMBO

Outdoor Spinning Ride — est. — **1955** *Lively & Exciting*

★ # Dumbo the Flying Elephant

As a merry tune plays, Dumbo-shaped gondolas will take you up, up and away! You control the lever inside to make your vehicle skim close to the ground or soar up to the clouds. Once you're up there, take a second to notice what an amazing view you have of the Matterhorn— and all of Fantasyland! If you've wondered what it would be like to be a flying elephant, this is the ride for you!

HOT TIP Go behind the Dumbo ride to find an **extra Dumbo gondola**—it makes a great picture spot. **Smile!**

TIME MACHINE

1939	1941	1955	1955
Children's story "Dumbo" by Helen Aberson has just eight drawings.	*Disney's animated movie "Dumbo" stars a circus elephant & features the Casey Jr. Circus Train.*	*Casey Jr. Circus Train attraction is ready for riders a couple of weeks after Disneyland opens. Toot! Toot!*	*Dumbo the Flying Elephant becomes an instant Guest favorite when it opens a month after Opening Day.*

Casey Jr. Circus Train

ll aboard for a ride over hills and through valleys past the miniature *fairytale scenes* of Storybook Land. Will you ride in a fancy sleigh? An animal cage? Wherever you sit, Casey Jr. is ready to lead the way as his *toe-tapping* theme song plays. During your trip, he'll come to a hill he's not sure he can make it over but...he *thinks* he can, he *thinks* he can!

* OutDOOR Train RiDe * CALM & MeLLOW *
— est. —
1955

 HOT TIP This ride and **Storybook Land Canal Boats** are also fun at **night** when the tiny buildings and plants are lit up with **itty-bitty twinkling lights.**

SPY Take a close look—the **buildings** in Storybook Land are **handmade** and extremely **detailed.** Some of the doors can actually **open and close.**

FUN FACT

The sleigh-style train cars on the Casey Jr. Circus Train came from the antique carousel that was turned into King Arthur Carrousel.

WAY TO RECYCLE!

FUN FACT

This ride, inspired by the tea party scene in Disney's animated movie "Alice in Wonderland," is in every single Disney resort around the world.

TEATIME!

"Be patient is very good advice but the waiting makes me curious."
—ALICE

★ Mad Tea Party

Outdoor Spinning Ride • Lively & Exciting
—est.— 1955

Hop in a giant teacup and take a spin! You control how quickly you go with a wheel in the center of your teacup. Even if you don't spin your cup, you'll still turn a bit on the ride platform so get ready to get dizzy! The cute song you'll hear is a musical version of the Unbirthday Song from *Alice in Wonderland*. Just what exactly is an unbirthday? Well, you have one birthday a year but 364 unbirthdays. So, unless you're reading this on your birthday, a very merry unbirthday to you!

HOT TIP Hop in the **extra teacup** in front of The Mad Hatter shop for a **tea-tally** cute photo!

TIME MACHINE

1865
"Alice's Adventures in Wonderland" by Lewis Carroll is published.

1951
Disney's animated movie "Alice in Wonderland" hits theaters.

1955
"Clean cup! Move down!" Mad Tea Party is an Opening Day attraction in Disneyland.

1958
The Alice in Wonderland ride opens.

★ Alice in Wonderland

 MAY BE SCARY

Climb into a caterpillar and follow the White Rabbit to the wild, wacky world of Wonderland!

You'll see singing flowers, the curious Caterpillar and the grinning Cheshire Cat. Next, it's on to the Royal Rose Garden where an army of playing cards are painting the roses red for that grumpy Queen of Hearts. When she shouts "Off with their heads!" you'll escape and zigzag over to the Mad Hatter's colorful unbirthday party!

INDOOR DARK RIDE · Lively & exciting · est. 1958

 SPY
The giant mushroom near the entrance to this ride used to be a **ticket booth.** While on the ride, look down to spot the **Caterpillar's shoes** sitting on top!

FUN FACT

The building that the Alice in Wonderland ride is in is the SAME structure that Mr. Toad's Wild Ride is in. And you thought YOU had crazy neighbors!

HA HA!

FREQUENTLY ASKED QUESTIONS ABOUT tHE MAD HATTER

Q: Who is the Mad Hatter?
A: He is a zany character from *Alice in Wonderland*. He is actually called "The Hatter" in the original book by Lewis Carroll. A hatter was a maker or seller of hats.

Q: What is the "10/6" on his hat?
A: The card in his hat band is a price tag meaning the hat cost ten shillings and sixpence in old British money.

Q: Why is he angry?
A: In this case, "mad" means crazy. He got his name from an old-fashioned saying "as mad as a hatter." In the 1800s, hatters used a poisonous chemical called mercury while making hats. Over time, the exposure to mercury caused them to shake and have wild mood swings so people thought they were crazy.

FUN FACT

The Abominable Snowman—who was not in the Matterhorn ride until 1978—has been nicknamed Harold by Cast Members. He was given a makeover in 2015 as part of Disneyland's 60th Anniversary.

★ Matterhorn Bobsleds

Board a sleek bobsled for an exciting snowy adventure! You'll ZOOM past icy slopes, frozen cliffs, glittering crystal caves and cascading waterfalls on this high-speed thrill ride. But wait! What's that ominous growling sound you hear? It's the Abominable Snowman! As you race around corners and in and out of dark tunnels, you never know where you may meet him. If you can escape his clutches, you'll splash down in an alpine lake and live to tell the tale!

HOT TIP There are **two separate lines** that will give you two different trips through the mountain. See which one you like best!

ROLLER COASTER
—est.—
1959
WILD & THRILLING

TIME MACHINE

1955
Disneyland opens with Holiday Hill, made from dirt dug up to build the moat around Sleeping Beauty Castle.

1958
"Third Man on the Mountain" filmed in Switzerland inspires Walt Disney to make the Matterhorn ride.

1959
The world's first tubular steel roller coaster opens where Holiday Hill used to be—Matterhorn Bobsleds!

1994
Au revoir! The Skyway gondolas that travel through the Matterhorn are removed.

Fun Facts about The Matterhorn

The real Matterhorn mountain in Europe's Alps mountain range is about a hundred times taller than the one in Disneyland.

The Skyway ride used to pass through the Matterhorn. When the Skyway closed, most of the tunnels were filled in.

The Matterhorn's peak is the highest point in the park.

When Tinker Bell flies across Disneyland during nighttime shows, she starts on the Matterhorn & ends at Sleeping Beauty Castle.

The snow on the mountain is made from glass beads that reflect the sunlight just like real snow.

Look up! Sometimes there are real mountain climbers on the Matterhorn.

A small basketball court was set up inside the top part of the mountain for Cast Members.

The Wells Expedition supplies seen inside the ride honor Frank Wells who was a mountain climber, skier & the President of the Disney Company.

Permanecer sentados por favor.

Disney fans love the safety announcement on this ride, which was recorded by the original Voice of Disneyland, Jack Wagner. In "Toy Story 2," Tour Guide Barbie actually says this same announcement.

FUN FacT

It's a Small World get its flair from Disney artist Mary Blair. To honor Mary, Imagineers made a doll flying a red balloon from the Eiffel Tower look like her.

BONJOUR!

★ It's a Small World

Climb aboard for "the happiest cruise that ever sailed 'round the world." You'll travel by boat past hundreds of children dressed in the traditional clothing of their homelands, including Scotland, India, Brazil, Australia and many other countries. The darling dolls sing the ride's theme song in many different languages—one of the catchiest tunes ever in the history of history. There's even a bubbly version sung by mermaids! You just can't visit Disneyland and NOT go on this classic ride but, watch out, you might get the song stuck in your head for the rest of the day!

HOT TIP It's a Small World's incredible **clock tower** outside the ride actually opens up every **15 minutes** and puts on quite a show!

SPY The gold you see on the outside of this ride is **real 22-karat gold.** Ka-ching!

INDOOR Boat Ride
— est. —
1966
Calm & Mellow

TIME MACHINE

1964
Disney creates It's A Small World for the New York World's Fair.

1966
It's A Small World moves across the country to open in Disneyland.

1997
The ride starts getting in the Christmas spirit with annual decorations, lights & a Christmas music medley. Ho, Ho, Ho!

2009
Disney characters like Donald Duck, Mulan & Sheriff Woody are added to the ride.

"It's a small world but I wouldn't want to paint it."
—STEVEN WRIGHT

Photographs by Dave DeCaro • http://davelandweb.com | Abominable snowman illustration by Lindsay Gibson • www.etsy.com/shop/emandsprout

FUN FACT
Figaro the Cat is best known for his first appearance in the movie "Pinocchio" but he also appeared in many short cartoons as the pet of Minnie Mouse.

ME WOW!

> "You buttered your bread. Now sleep in it!"
> —JIMINY CRICKET

★ # Food & Drinks

EDELWEISS SNACKS

Named after the small edelweiss flowers that grow on the real Matterhorn mountain in Switzerland, this charming alpine chalet serves up on-the-go snacks so hearty you can call them a meal.

• *Chimichangas* • *Corn on the cob* • *Turkey legs*

HOT TIP Enjoy your Edelweiss snacks on the **former boat dock** across the way near the water. It's a peaceful spot that many people don't know about.

HEY KIDS COLOR ME IN!

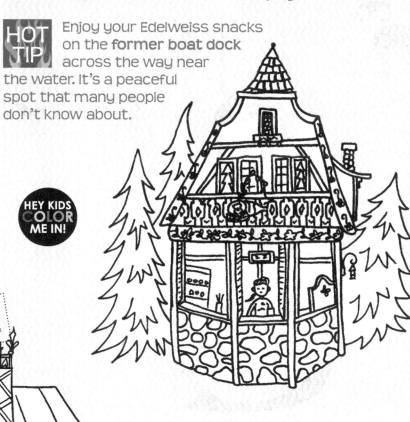

TROUBADOUR TAVERN

Hungry knights, wandering minstrels and damsels in distress can stop by this medieval pavilion-style stand for hearty snacks and treats. Troubadours recited poems and sang songs in the Middle Ages so if you really love your food, go ahead and sing about it!

• *Bratwurst*
• *Pretzel bites*
• *Stuffed baked potatoes*

GROWL!

Village Haus Restaurant

This storybook setting offers a cobblestone patio outside or four Pinocchio-themed rooms inside—the Cleo Room, the Jiminy Cricket Room, the Stromboli Room or Geppetto's Workshop. What does "Haus" mean? House, in German!

• *Hamburgers* • *Pizza* • *Salads*

SPY Many buildings in Disneyland have cute **weather vanes!** Look up and you'll see a crocodile, a whale, a ship and many more!

What do Imagineers do when a sign is installed off-center? They get creative!

Roastie-Toasties!

Cute **popcorn wagons** are all around Disneyland. Each one matches the area it sits in, right down to the dolls called **Roastie-Toasties** who turn the cranks to churn the popcorn. Look for these hardworking little guys when you're in the park. Put a ✓ next to the ones you find.

LAND:	ROASTIE-TOASTIE:
Fantasyland	☐ Abominable Snowman
Main Street	☐ Circus Clown
Mickey's Toontown	☐ Train Conductor
Tomorrowland	☐ Astronaut

Did you see any others? What did they look like?

"Come now, dry those tears. You can't go to the ball looking like that."
—FAIRY GODMOTHER

MAGICAL MAKEOVER

Fairy Godmothers are standing by to transform girls into glamorous princesses with a fancy hairstyle, makeup, nail polish and more at the salon in the back of **Bibbidi Bobbidi Boutique.** For boys, the Knight Package offers young heroes a dashing, slicked back hairstyle, sword and shield IF they can fight their way past all the princess products up front!

SPY Look on the outside of this boutique to find some very special beams featuring **Captain Hook, Smee** and the **Croc** from *Peter Pan!*

MOUSE EAR HAT

The Mad Hatter sells the #1 Disneyland souvenir of all time: mouse ear hats! These cute hats were inspired by a cartoon where Mickey Mouse tipped his ears to Minnie. First made in basic black, these hats now come in a huge variety of colors and styles and many can be custom embroidered.

HOT TIP You can buy **Mouse Ear hats** at other shops and stands around the park but not all locations offer embroidery.

WORDLY DOLL

The super-cute dolls inside **It's a Small World Toy Shop** are dressed in traditional outfits from various countries just like the super-cute dolls in the It's a Small World ride.

YOUR COAT OF ARMS

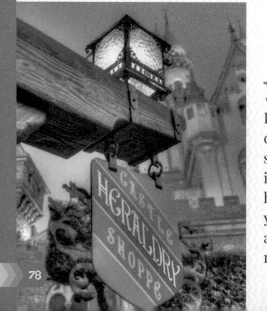

In medieval times, families and clans created symbols called "coats of arms" which they would paint on shields and wear on tunic shirts over their armor to identify themselves in battle. Find out if your family has a coat of arms and have it printed on the item of your choice at the **Castle Heraldry Shoppe** which also carries collectible swords, shields and other royal goods.

Photograph by Dave DeCaro • http://www.daveelandweb.com

GUESS THE COAT OF ARMS!

These shields belong to **Captain Hook, Gaston** and **Elsa.** Write the character's name in the box below their coat of arms. *Answers on page 181.*

Have fun **making up** your own coat of arms below! Write your last name in the ribbon banner at the bottom of the shield, then draw things that are important to you in **each of the four sections.** Use your initials, your favorite colors or anything you like!

The prince from Snow White and the Seven Dwarfs

The mighty Matterhorn mountain looms behind the clock tower above the entrance to Peter Pan's Flight.

MICKEY'S TOONTOWN

What Will You Find in This Land?

ATTRACTIONS
- Chip 'n Dale Treehouse
- Disneyland Railroad
- Donald's Boat
- Gadget's Go Coaster
- Goofy's Playhouse
- Mickey's House
- Minnie's House
- Roger Rabbit's Car Toon Spin

FOOD & DRINKS
- Clarabelle's
- Daisy's Diner
- Pluto's Dog House

SHOPS
- Gag Factory - Toontown Five & Dime

MEET N' GREETS
- Mickey Mouse

ALSO IN THIS CHAPTER
- Top 4 Disneyland Inventions
- Tons of Interactive Fun!
- Make Your Own Cartoon Strips!

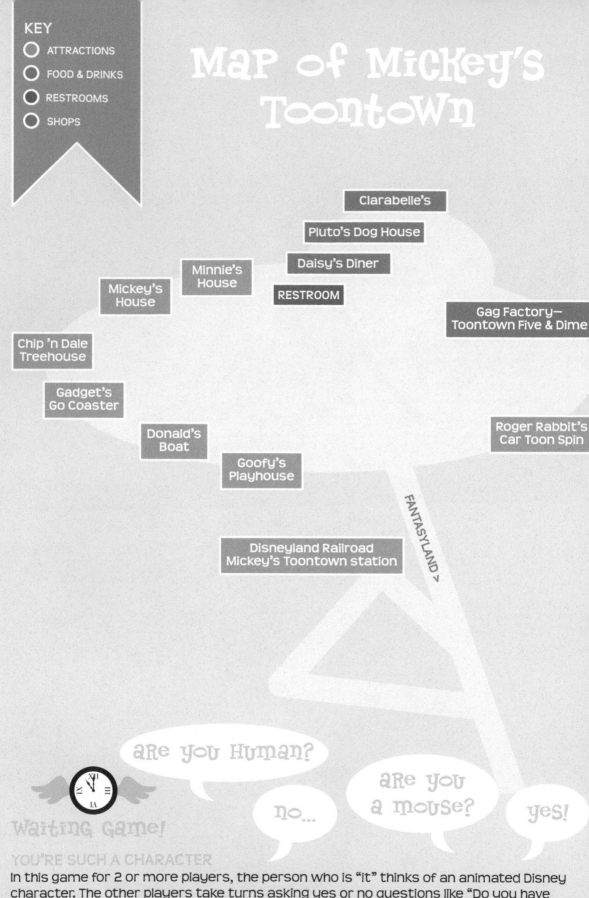

Map of Mickey's Toontown

KEY
- ATTRACTIONS
- FOOD & DRINKS
- RESTROOMS
- SHOPS

Clarabelle's

Pluto's Dog House

Daisy's Diner

Minnie's House

RESTROOM

Mickey's House

Gag Factory—
Toontown Five & Dime

Chip 'n Dale Treehouse

Gadget's
Go Coaster

Donald's
Boat

Roger Rabbit's
Car Toon Spin

Goofy's
Playhouse

FANTASYLAND

Disneyland Railroad
Mickey's Toontown station

are you Human?

no...

are you
a mouse?

yes!

Waiting Game!

YOU'RE SUCH A CHARACTER

In this game for 2 or more players, the person who is "it" thinks of an animated Disney character. The other players take turns asking yes or no questions like "Do you have magical powers?" or "Are you male?" If someone can guess the character, they win. If no one can guess who the character is, the person who is it wins.

Walk into a Cartoon

Where do cartoon characters live? In Toontown, where "Toons" rule. If you could really be in a cartoon, it'd be a lot like walking into Mickey's Toontown. This area is filled with curvy buildings, whimsical painted hills and trees, and attractions related to Disney cartoon characters like Mickey Mouse, Donald Duck and Goofy. Mickey's Toontown sometimes opens later and closes earlier than the rest of the park, so be sure to check the schedule!

HOT TIP Unlike most of Disneyland's lands which flow into **other sections** of the park, **Mickey's Toontown** is a **dead end** so, once you've had your fun, you'll turn around and go back out **the way you came in.**

★ Mickey's House

Go on in and take a peek around Mickey Mouse's cute little house! You'll see his living room, den, laundry room and backyard with a vegetable garden and Pluto's doghouse. Then, it's on to Mickey's barn which he's turned into a movie studio. Catch some classic Mickey Mouse cartoon clips in the Screening Room before you meet the mouse himself!

INDOOR WALK-THROUGH * MELLOW & CALM *
— est. —
1993

SPY
See if you can spot a **picture** of Mickey with his pal **Walt Disney** inside Mickey's place.

FUN FACT

In 1978, Mickey Mouse was the first cartoon character to get a star on the Hollywood Walk of Fame.

STAR POWER!

MICKEY MOUSE

★ Meet n' Greets

You can meet Mickey Mouse behind his house in the Movie Barn. He can't wait to meet you, pose for pictures and give you a big, warm hug!

TIME MACHINE

1928
The first Mickey Mouse cartoon is released, starring Mickey & Minnie Mouse!

1929
Mickey wears his famous white gloves for the first time.

1955
Hey there! Hi there! Ho there! "The Mickey Mouse Club" TV show is first aired.

1993
Mickey's Toontown opens with Mickey's House & Minnie's House as the main attractions.

★ Minnie's House

INDOOR WALK-THROUGH ★ CALM & MELLOW ★ 1993

Stroll through the *super-sweet* home of Mickey's favorite gal—Minnie Mouse! Inside the house, you can try out Minnie's chair or *relax* on her glamorous lounge. Stop by Minnie's desk and read her email—she won't mind. The fun continues in her *kitchen* where you can take a seat at the cute table, peek inside the *Cheesemore* fridge, twist a dial to make a cake rise in the oven and turn on the dishwasher. Out the back door you'll find a darling *wishing well* and a rose-covered *gazebo* where Minnie Mouse likes to sometimes unwind and visit with Guests.

HOT TIP The cookies on Minnie's kitchen table are actually a **hologram.** No matter how you try to grab them, you never can because they're **not really there!**

SO YOU KNOW... **hologram** = a projected 3-D image

FUN FACT
Minnie's full name is Minerva Mouse.

MINERVA?!

Minnie is often found behind her house in her girly gazebo!

"Yaaaaaa-hoo-
hoo-hoo-hooey!"
—GOOFY

★ Climb-Around Fun

GooFy's PLayHouse

Thing are all crazy at Goofy's place!
Explore his wacky garden, then find more
silly fun inside. Try out Goofy's fun piano
and have a seat in one of his big chairs.

 SPY Look up to the roof of Goofy's
Playhouse to see his **big,
green hat!**

CHiP 'n DaLe TReeHouse

This treehouse isn't built **on** a tree, it's
built **in** a tree! Scamper upstairs and
down just like a playful chipmunk.

HOT TIP Which chipmunk is which?
Dale has bangs and Chip has a
dark nose like a chocolate chip.

DonaLD's Boat

Climb aboard this colorful boat named
Miss Daisy after Donald's favorite
female fowl. Give the steering
wheel a spin, ring the bell and
pull the ship's whistle!

 SPY Check out **Donald's
sailor suit and hat**
on the clothesline.

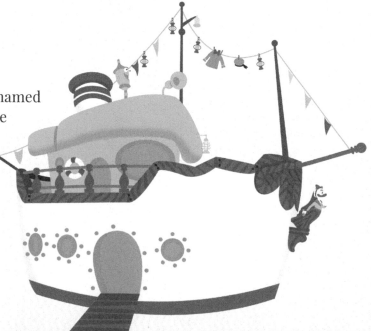

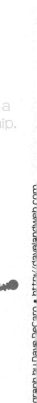

> "If they'd straightened out the angle on that last curve, we'd have seen some real speed!"
> —GADGET HACKWRENCH

★ Gadget's Go Coaster

Roller Coaster * est. * 1993 * Lively & exciting

Gadget Hackwrench is an inventor and a friend to Chip 'n Dale. She's known for her brilliant inventions made from everyday objects. With her *bright ideas,* tools and things she's found lying around, she's put together this *clever coaster.* You'll leave from Gadget's Workshop and climb into into an *acorn train* to wind up, down and all around Toon Lake.

SPY Look out for **funny frogs** who'll try to squirt a stream of water at you!

FUN FACT
The letters on the sign for Gadget's Go Coaster are made from objects like a wrench, hammer & coiled spring.

GENIUS!

TOP 4 DISNEYLAND INVENTIONS

The Disney Company has always been filled with **unbelievably creative people** just like Walt Disney—and **Gadget Hackwrench!** Here are some cool **inventions** that have been dreamed up for Disneyland:

#1 Go Away Green—muted paint color blends objects into the background
#2 Tubular Steel Roller Coaster—Matterhorn Bobsleds was the first
#3 Audio-Animatronics—these robots make attractions way more fun
#4 Doritos—crispy chips made from leftover tortillas were a huge hit

TIME MACHINE

1947
Chip 'n Dale terrorize poor Pluto in their first appearance—a cartoon called "Private Pluto."

1951
The chipmunks get their own cartoon series but only three episodes are made. Nuts!

1988
The "Chip 'n Dale Rescue Rangers" TV show begins, featuring a mouse character named Gadget.

1993
Mickey's Toontown opens with Gadget's Go Coaster.

FUN FACT

The dreaded Dip that the Toons are so afraid of is made of turpentine, benzene & acetone. Those three liquids are actually used to remove paint from cartoon cels, so the Dip really is deadly to a Toon.

OUCH!

"I'm not bad. I'm just drawn that way."
—JESSICA RABBIT

★ Roger Rabbit's Car Toon Spin

INDOOR DARK RIDE
—est.—
1994
Lively & Exciting

Hop behind the wheel of Lenny the Cab to take a spin through Toontown on a hare-raising adventure with Roger Rabbit, whose wife Jessica has been kidnapped. Watch out for the naughty Weasels dumping deadly Dip in the road—a glowing goo that makes your car skid out of control. Spin the steering wheel and make your cab twist and turn all the way around as you crash through a china shop, an explosive power plant, and the Gag Factory. Will you make it out in one piece? Never fear, Roger Rabbit will show up in time to save the day with a portable hole and you don't even have to say "P-p-p-lease!"

SPY When you're in **line** for this ride, be sure to look for the funny **license plates** hanging on the wall.

19 TOONTOWN 35
2N TOWN

19 TOONTOWN 42
CAP 10 HK

19 TOONTOWN 45
1DRLND

TIME MACHINE

1981
"Who Censored Roger Rabbit?" by Gary K. Wolf is published.

1988
A combo of live-action & animation, "Who Framed Roger Rabbit" hits theaters.

1989
"Tummy Trouble," the first of three short cartoons starring Roger Rabbit is released.

1994
Roger Rabbit's Car Toon Spin opens in Mickey's Toontown. Jeepers!

Tons of interactive Fun!

There are many **entertaining spots** in Mickey's Toontown. As you explore the fire station, post office, gas station and other businesses, you'll find lots of things to **pull, poke,** or **listen to** or **see.** Put a ✔ next to the ones you try!

☐ Try to pry the top off the **wooden crates** near the Fireworks Factory

☐ Squeeze through the **bars** at the Dog Pound

☐ Watch the **Clockenspiel** above Toontown's City Hall at the top of the hour

☐ Look for the **"blank" sign** that starts with the words "THIS IS A BLANK SIGN!"

☐ Push down the **plunger** outside the Fireworks Factory

☐ Press the **doorbell** at the Toontown Glass Works

☐ Get a drink from the **water fountains** at Goofy's Gas Station

☐ Check the **mailboxes** in the Post Office

Did you find any others? If so, list them here:

_____

_____

_____

_____

Disneyland Railroad

Mickey's Toontown is one of the four stops on the Disneyland Railroad.
More info on page 44.

MICKEY'S TOONTOWN

NEW ORLEANS SQUARE

TOMORROWLAND

MAIN STREET USA

Fun Fact
The Toontown train station (above) is made to look like a cartoon version of the New Orleans Square station (below).

NEAT!

FUN FACT

Pluto is one of the "Fab Five" Disney characters which also includes:
Mickey Mouse
Minnie Mouse
Donald Duck
& Goofy.

FAB!

MINI QUIZ!

Can you guess which of these characters appeared in a cartoon first?
Answer on page 181.
☐ Clarabelle
☐ Daisy
☐ Pluto

 ★ **Food & Drinks**

HOT TIP Toontown's restaurants are all **quick service** and all share the same **outdoor seating area.**

DAISY'S DINER

Daisy Duck's dining spot keeps it simple, serving up what kids love most—pizza!
• *Cheese pizza* • *Pepperoni pizza*

PLUTO'S DOG HOUSE

This home for hot dogs looks just like the doghouse where Mickey's pet dog Pluto lives.
• *Hot dogs* • *Macaroni* • *Turkey sandwiches*

CLARABELLE'S

Look for a white awning with black and cow spots and you've found Clarabelle's. Named after one of Minnie Mouse's friends, this eatery has a cute weather vane on top shaped like Clarabelle Cow holding two cones of frozen yogurt.
• *Salads* • *Turkey sandwiches* • *Yogurt parfaits*

Make your own cartoon strips!

Walt Disney loved to draw **cartoons**. Now it's your turn to be the artist! Draw a **three-panel comic** in each of the three rows below about your adventures in Disneyland. Write the title of each cartoon above each strip and sign the bottom right corner of the last panel. Your main characters can be people, animals or even objects.

TITLE: _____

TITLE: _____

TITLE: _____

Mickey Mouse conducts the fun from the top of this musical fountain in Mickey's Toontown.

TOMORROWLAND

What Will You Find in This Land?

ENTERTAINMENT
- Jedi Training Academy
- Special Screenings

ATTRACTIONS
- Astro Orbitor
- Autopia
- Buzz Lightyear Astro Blasters
- Disneyland Monorail
- Disneyland Railroad
- Finding Nemo Submarine Voyage
- Space Mountain
- Star Tours—The Adventures Continue
- Star Wars Launch Bay
- Super Hero HQ

FOOD & DRINKS
- Redd Rockett's Pizza Port
- Tomorrowland Terrace

SHOPS
- Little Green Men Store Command
- Spaceport Document Control
- The Star Trader
- TomorrowLanding

MEET N' GREETS
- Spider-Man
- Star Wars Characters
- Thor

ALSO IN THIS CHAPTER
- Star Wars Character Quiz!
- Have a Ball in Tomorrowland
- Imagineers at Play
- Unique Souvenirs
- Talk Like an Astronaut!

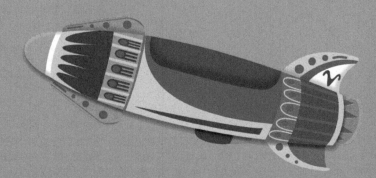

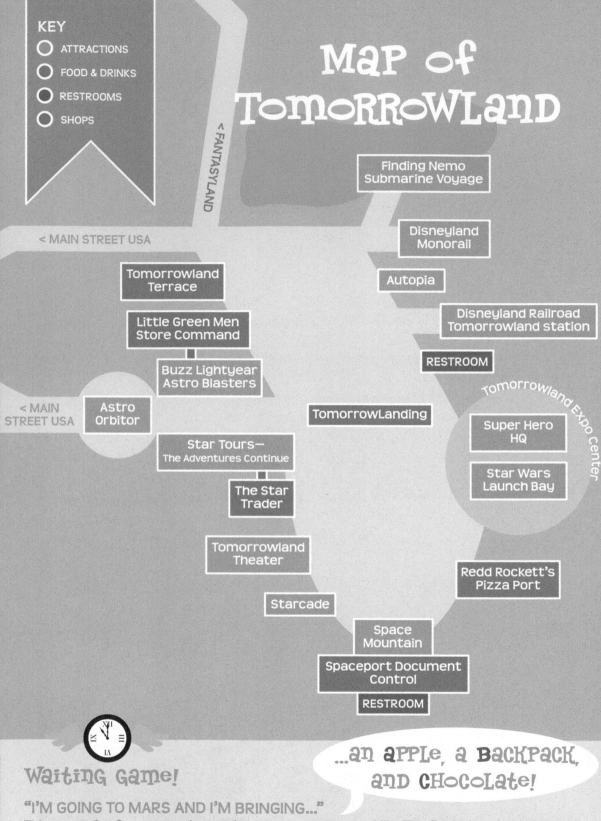

MAP of TOMORROWLAND

KEY
- ○ ATTRACTIONS
- ○ FOOD & DRINKS
- ● RESTROOMS
- ○ SHOPS

< FANTASYLAND

< MAIN STREET USA

Finding Nemo Submarine Voyage

Disneyland Monorail

Tomorrowland Terrace

Autopia

Little Green Men Store Command

Disneyland Railroad Tomorrowland station

RESTROOM

Buzz Lightyear Astro Blasters

Tomorrowland Expo Center

< MAIN STREET USA

Astro Orbitor

TomorrowLanding

Super Hero HQ

Star Tours—The Adventures Continue

Star Wars Launch Bay

The Star Trader

Tomorrowland Theater

Redd Rockett's Pizza Port

Starcade

Space Mountain

Spaceport Document Control

RESTROOM

Waiting Game!

...an apple, a backpack, and chocolate!

"I'M GOING TO MARS AND I'M BRINGING..."

This game for 2 or more players tests your memory skills. The first player starts by adding something that starts with the letter **A** to the sentence. For example: "I'm going to Mars and I'm bringing an **apple** with me." The next player repeats the sentence and adds something that starts with the letter **B**—for example, "I'm going to Mars and I'm bringing an apple and a **backpack** with me." The next player adds something that starts with the letter **C** and so on. If anyone can't remember the items correctly, they are out. Whoever can make it to the end of the alphabet without forgetting any of the items wins.

Great Big Beautiful Tomorrow

When Tomorrowland first opened in 1955 it was made to look like a vision of the far, far future—1986! This land has had major changes over the years to keep it looking ultramodern and it looks totally different from when it first opened. In fact, only one original attraction still stands today—Autopia. The tall rocket ships, streamlined space stations, modern arches and sleek Monorail gliding overhead will make you feel like you're in a futuristic city that's simply out of this world!

 Disney Imagineers believe **open space** will become rarer in the future and that food will have to be grown in any available spot. Because of this, Tomorrowland's **landscaping** is filled with **fruits and vegetables.**

★ Entertainment

For showtimes, pick up an Entertainment Times Guide at the Main Entrance, get info at City Hall or ask a friendly Cast Member.

• **Jedi Training Academy**—interactive *Star Wars*-themed show on Tomorrowland Terrace Stage
• **Special Screenings**—limited engagements of short films, sneak peeks of new movies, and classic clips shown at Tomorrowland Theater

FUN FACT

1995's "Toy Story," where audiences first met Space Ranger Buzz Lightyear & Sheriff Woody, was the first full-length movie made totally on computers.

STELLAR!

"There seems to be no sign of intelligent life anywhere."
—BUZZ LIGHTYEAR

★ Buzz Lightyear Astro Blasters

INDOOR DARK RIDE — est. — 2005 — Lively & exciting

Blast into Buzz Lightyear's world in this mega-colorful, shooting gallery ride. You'll feel like you've shrunk down to the size of an action figure when you pass by the oversized objects to board an XP-40 Space Cruiser. Your mission is to defeat the evil Emperor Zurg by zapping the Z targets. You'll use a joystick to spin into position and a laser cannon to try and hit as many targets as you can. At the end of the ride, check your score on the dashboard of the cruiser and compare it to the rankings on the status board on the wall. Will you be a Star Cadet or rule the galaxy as a Galactic Hero?

HOT TIP If the ride stops while you're on it, **consider it a bonus.** The lasers and targets usually keep working so you can **keep racking up points!**

SPY While you're busy **saving the universe,** your photo will be taken! Email it to anyone you like for **free** near the attraction's exit.

TIME MACHINE

1955
The Circarama theater opens where Buzz Lightyear Astro Blasters is now.

1995
"Toy Story" hits theaters & is the first of many full-length & short movies starring Buzz & Woody.

1998
Buzz Lightyear's Space Ranger Spin in Disney's Magic Kingdom in Florida is the first Buzz Lightyear-themed ride.

2005
Disneyland's Buzz Lightyear Astro Blasters opens. What a blast!

SO YOU KNOW...
orbit = travel around something

★ Astro Orbitor

Outdoor Spinning Ride ★ Lively & Exciting ★
est. 1998

Climb aboard a high-flying, retro rocket to *orbit* around a galaxy of golden planets. You control how high you fly by **pulling** and **pushing** the lever inside your rocket. Skim the ground or soar above the crowds for an *aerial* view of Tomorrowland and beyond!

 HOT TIP

Astro Orbitor is decorated with the twelve **astrological symbols.** Your astrological "sign" is based on when your **birthday** is. Circle your sign below and see if you can snag a ride on the rocket with your sign on it!

♈ March 21–April 19 Aries	♌ July 23–Aug. 22 Leo	⟷ Nov. 22–Dec. 21 Sagitarius
♉ April 20–May 20 Taurus	♍ Aug. 23–Sept. 22 Virgo	♑ Dec. 22–Jan. 19 Capricorn
♊ May 21–June 20 Gemini	♎ Sept. 23–Oct. 22 Libra	♒ Jan. 20–Feb. 18 Aquarius
♋ June 21–July 22 Cancer	♏ Oct. 23–Nov. 21 Scorpio	♓ Feb. 19–March 20 Pisces

FUN FACT

The look of Astro Orbitor is inspired by Italian artist Leonardo da Vinci's drawings of an astrolabe—a tool for figuring out the height of the sun & stars. Born in 1452, da Vinci is also known for painting the Mona Lisa.

ARTSY!

"A well-spent day brings happy sleep."
—LEONARDO DA VINCI

TIME MACHINE

1956
Astro-Jets opens & riders rotate around a red & white control tower.

1964
Astro-Jets changes its name to Tomorrowland Jets.

1967
Tomorrowland Jets are replaced by sleek, white Rocket Jets, which close in 1997.

1998
Tomorrowland gets a new spinning rocket ride when Astro Orbitor opens. Whee!

FUN FACT

A form of the phrase "I have a bad feeling about this" is said in every Star Wars movie.

NO WAY!

"Why you stuck-up, half-witted, scruffy-looking nerf herder!"
—PRINCESS LEIA

★ Star Tours
—The Adventures Continue

FLIGHT SIMULATOR
—est.—
1987
WILD & THRILLING

Wind through a busy spaceport just like you might see in a *Star Wars* movie to catch a ride on a StarSpeeder 1000 starship. Once aboard, you'll strap in to get ready to explore a variety of intergalactic destinations. When members of the evil Imperial army attempt to search the starship for a rebel spy, C-3PO—who was sitting in the pilot's seat to do some maintenance work—is forced to rocket the StarSpeeder to an exciting escape. The state-of-the-art technology on this ride can mix and match the stories into over 50 possible combinations, so you'll never know where you're headed next. Maybe you'll see the icy cliffs of Hoth, the underwater cities of Naboo, the desert landscapes of Tatooine, the woodlands of Kashyyyk, the busy sky traffic of Coruscant, or even the menacing Death Star. Can you escape the dark side and make it safely to the next spaceport? May the Force be with you.

HOT TIP

The **C-3PO** and **R2-D2** robots you walk past in the line for Star Tours are **actual props** from the Star Wars movies!

SPY

Also in the line, a **droid** is scanning luggage—see if there's **anything odd** in the bags he's checking.

TIME MACHINE

1977
Princess Leia, Luke Skywalker & Han Solo battle Darth Vader in the first Star Wars movie.

1985
Adventure Thru Inner Space, where riders shrink smaller than an atom, closes to make way for Star Tours.

1987
Yes! Star Tours opens in Disneyland to transport space tourists to a galaxy far, far away.

2011
Star Tours reopens as Star Tours—The Adventures Continue with all-new stories & special effects.

STAR WARS CHARACTER QUIZ!

Think you know your *Star Wars* characters? Draw a line connecting the character's name to the close-up image of their outfit. The first one's been done for you. *Answers on page 181.*

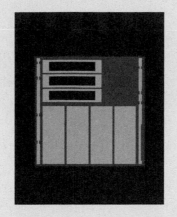

C-3PO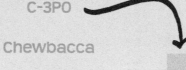

Chewbacca

Darth Vader

Han Solo

Luke Skywalker

R2-D2

Stormtrooper

Yoda

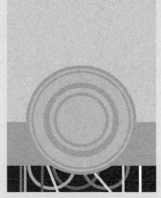

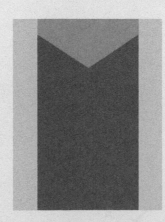

★ Finding Nemo Submarine Voyage

Submarine Ride ★ est. 2007 ★ Lively & Exciting

Dive into an Australian harbor in a **bright yellow submarine** on an underwater research expedition! As you peek through your porthole, you'll see characters from the animated movie **Finding Nemo** having all sorts of adventures. You'll cruise past a sea of jellyfish, an underwater volcano and more before you come across a hungry whale who thinks your sub looks like a tasty snack!

HOT TIP If you notice passengers on the opposite side of the sub are seeing **different things,** don't worry! Both sides eventually pass the same sights.

SPY Look for the **name** of your sub on the side. Will you ride in the Argonaut, Explorer, Mariner, Nautilus, Neptune, Seafarer, Scout or Voyager?

FUN FACT

The theme of the first version of Submarine Voyage was a trip from Hawaii to the North Pole. Passengers saw a giant squid, a sea serpent, mermaids & more.

COOL!

Mine! Mine! Mine!

MARINER 407

TIME MACHINE

1955	1959	2003	2007
Tomorrowland Boats attraction opens in the lagoon that will later be home to Submarine Voyage.	*Submarine Voyage opens in Disneyland & closes in 1998. Dive! Dive! Dive!*	*The Disney•Pixar movie "Finding Nemo" hits theaters.*	*The submarine attraction reopens as Finding Nemo Submarine Voyage.*

Disneyland Monorail

SO YOU KNOW...
mono = one

Single-Rail Train
est. 1959
Calm & Mellow

The only place to catch a ride on the Monorail *inside* Disneyland is at the Tomorrowland station. The Monorail uses *clean* electrical energy to glide smoothly above the ground on an elevated *single-rail track* at about thirty miles per hour. This futuristic transportation system takes you *out of Disneyland* past Disney California Adventure and the Grand Californian hotel to the Downtown Disney station near the Disneyland Hotel. You can hop on for a *one-way trip* or see if *round trips* are available that day so you can end up right back where you started. Ask nicely and you may be allowed to ride up front with the driver!

HOT TIP Be sure to get your **hand stamped** and have your **admission ticket** with you if you leave the park on the Monorail and are planning to come back in!

RATE THIS ATTRACTION
- ☐ Never. Again.
- ☐ Not so hot.
- ☐ Pretty cool...
- ☐ Way cool!
- ☐ Awesome!!
- ☐ AHH, MY FAVE!!!

One word I'd use to describe this attraction:
_____

FUN FACT
Legendary Disney Imagineer Bob Gurr designed many of the vehicles in Disneyland including the Matterhorn's Bobsleds, Autopia's cars & Disneyland Monorail.

VROOM!

TOMORROWLAND

DOWNTOWN DISNEY

Mini Quiz!
Can you guess which one of these people came to the Monorail's dedication ceremony?
Answer on page 181.
☐ Elvis Presley ☐ Richard Nixon ☐ Mark Twain

TIME MACHINE

1958	1959	1961	2000
On a trip to Germany, Walt Disney notices the ALWEG Monorail & decides it's just what Tomorrowland needs.	*Disneyland Monorail opens for passengers in Disneyland. Smooth move!*	*The Monorail becomes more than just a sightseeing ride when a second station opens at Disneyland Hotel.*	*A brand new Downtown Disney station replaces the Disneyland Hotel station.*

Whee!

RATE THIS ATTRACTION
- ☐ Never. Again.
- ☐ Not so hot.
- ☐ Pretty cool...
- ☐ Way cool!
- ☐ Awesome!!
- ☐ AHH, MY FAVE!!!

One word I'd use to describe this attraction:

_ _ _ _ _ _ _ _ _ _ _ _

FUN FACT

Disneyland has had oodles of Autopia rides: Fantasyland Autopia, Junior Autopia, Midget Autopia & Tomorrowland Autopia.

HONK! HONK!

"A motorcar! Gad, what have I been missing!"
—MR. TOAD

★ Autopia

SO YOU KNOW...
utopia = an ideal place

outdoor car ride ★ —est.— **1955** ★ *lively & exciting*

What kid doesn't dream of driving their own car? At Autopia that dream comes true when you hop behind the wheel of your very own gas-powered coupe, off-road vehicle or sports car. To go, put the pedal to the metal. To stop or slow down, release the same pedal. Be ready because it is NOT too easy to get that pedal down—you've got to use your muscles AND the muscles on your muscles too. Once you've got the hang of it, you'll enjoy a joyful jaunt around the winding, scenic roads of Autopia!

HOT TIP
Be sure to pick up a **FREE driver's license** on Autopia! Take it home to add your **photo,** OR use a photo booth near the ride's exit **for a fee.**

SPY
While driving down the lanes of Autopia, look for a sign that says **Route 55**—a nod to the fact that this attraction opened in **1955.**

Photograph by Dave DeCaro • http://daveland.web.com

TIME MACHINE

1955
Autopia is an Opening Day attraction in Disneyland.

1965
A center guide rail is installed on Autopia. Safety first!

1967
Autopia's cars are redesigned to look like convertible Corvette Stingrays.

2000
Autopia is revamped with a bigger track & all-new cars—Suzy the coupe, Dusty the off-road vehicle & Sparky the sports car.

★ Tomorrowland Expo Center

Star Wars Launch Bay

This must-visit destination for *Star Wars* fans features special exhibits, videogames and chances to meet characters from the Light Side or the Dark Side—if you dare!

Super Hero HQ

This headquarters for superhero fans has a Game Center with new videogames to try out, superhero souvenirs and opportunities to meet your favorite hero in person. You can even feel like a superhero yourself inside the Hall of Armor where you can virtually suit up as Iron Man.

Spidey

FUN FACT
Thor's magical hammer returns to him like a boomerang when he throws it & actually has a name —Mjolnir.

BY THE POWER OF THOR!

★ Meet n' Greets

Tomorrowland has three official Meet n' Greets. Spider-Man and Thor are in Super Hero HQ and Star Wars Characters can be found inside Star Wars Launch Bay.

TIME MACHINE

1967
A rotating theater opens with an Audio-Animatronic show called Carousel of Progress.

1974
The show changes its tune & becomes America Sings. Joy to the world!

1998
The theater is transformed into an exhibit hall called Innoventions.

2015
The building is revamped & reopens as Tomorrowland Expo Center.

★ Space Mountain

ROLLER COASTER * WILD & THRILLING * —EST.— 1977

Towering over Tomorrowland, this **indoor roller coaster** is one of Disneyland's most thrilling, high-speed rides. You'll wind through a *futuristic* space station to reach the loading dock where you'll board your *rocket.* As you click-click-click your way uphill into the darkness, the speakers in your seat will countdown to BLAST OFF! Hold on tight as your rocket speedily spirals through the darkest depths of *outerspace* while a groovy galactic soundtrack plays. Whizzing past planets, stars, meteors and comets, you'll suddenly *blast* into a tunnel of light to find yourself back in the loading dock thinking either "I survived!" or "Again! Again! Again!"

 HOT TIP The blast of light near the end of this ride is a **camera flash.** You can buy a print at **Spaceport Document Control** near Space Mountain's exit.

FuN FaCT
A real astronaut helped design Space Mountain! Gordon Cooper went to outerspace on the Mercury-Atlas 9 & Gemini 5, & later went to Anaheim to help make the ride as realistic as possible.

MISSION ACCOMPLISHED!

"SS-77, this is Mission Control. We are initiating power transfer in three, two, one..."
—SPACE MOUNTAIN

Mini QuiZ!
Can you guess which one of these things you can do in space?
Answer on page 181.
☐ Burp ☐ Hear yourself scream ☐ Sneeze

TIME MACHINE

1964
Walt Disney has the idea for Space Mountain but they do NOT have the technology & the ride is put on hold.

1969
American astronauts Neil Armstrong & Buzz Aldrin are the first people to walk on the moon.

1975
If they can send a man to the moon, they can build Space Mountain. The ride premieres in Disney's Magic Kingdom in Florida.

1977
Space Mountain opens in Disneyland. Outta sight!

Fun Facts about Space Mountain

The number 77 can be seen in many spots in the hallways that lead to the loading dock. This number was used because the ride opened in 1977.

The ride building is 118 feet high, 200 feet wide & was built 2 stories into the ground.

Six of the original "Mercury Seven" United States astronauts attended the opening celebration for Space Mountain.

There are sometimes temporary themes with different music & special effects like "Space Mountain: Ghost Galaxy," "Rockin' Space Mountain" & the Star Wars-inspired "Hyperspace Mountain."

In 1997, the outside of Space Mountain was painted gold, copper, bronze & green! In 2003, it was changed back to the original white color.

In the 1990s, on-board ride music was added—a combo of of sci-fi & surf music that features famous surf guitarist Dick Dale.

Disneyland Railroad

Tomorrowland is one of the four stops on the Disneyland Railroad. *More info on page 44.*

MICKEY'S TOONTOWN

NEW ORLEANS SQUARE

TOMORROWLAND

MAIN STREET USA

SO YOU KNOW...
taxidermic = real animals that have been stuffed

FUN FACT

Impressive dioramas can be seen when you travel from Tomorrowland to Main Street USA on the train! These scenes have the park's only **taxidermic** animals & Audio-Animatronic dinosaurs.

ROAR!

★ Food & Drinks

Redd Rockett's Pizza Port

Refuel at this spaceport with indoor and outdoor seating offering Italian favorites served at walk-up stations.
• *Pasta* • *Pizza* • *Salads*

SPY Check out the retro **Moonliner III** rocket outside of Redd Rockett's place. To see the original rocket, check out the **vintage attraction posters** inside the restaurant.

Tomorrowland Terrace

This open-air, quick-service eatery has seating facing Tomorrowland Terrace Stage, which raises up out of the ground.
• *Breakfast burritos* • *Hamburgers* • *Salads*

Fun Fact
The story goes that Redd Rockett was a pilot & space trader who was tired of the bland food in outerspace & opened a chain of pizza joints.

TASTY!

Have a Ball in Tomorrowland

Sitting in front of Redd Rockett's Pizza Port is **Cosmic Waves.** This giant globe is something called a **Kugel ball**—a sculpture where a large sphere sits on a base supported by a thin layer of water. Even though the granite ball weighs **1,000 pounds,** you can easily move it because of how it's being supported by the water.

★ Unique Souvenirs

DROID IN A SOMBRERO

Design your own *Star Wars* droid in **The Star Trader.** Pick the body, arms, legs and head of your choice in the color you like and click them into place. There's even funny headgear like Mickey ears and Mexican sombrero hats.

TRICKED-OUT LIGHTSABER

Jedi Knights can build the lightsaber of their dreams at **The Star Trader.** Start with a single or double base and choose the color of your blade—or two blades if you have a double base. You can customize with different hilts, switches, hilt sleeves and caps too. Put it all together and you'll be ready for battle.

 Want a lightsaber like **Luke Skywalker's?** Choose a **blue blade.** For one like **Darth Vader's,** choose **red.**

Imagineers at Play

Tomorrowland's **Starcade** first opened in 1977 as a modern **videogame arcade.** Over the years, it changed to a mix of **retro games** and souvenirs and later hosted Meet n' Greets and special exhibits. Imagineers are hard at work creating **something new** for this spot. What will it be like? **It's a big mystery!** Was this open when you visited?
■ Yes   ■ No
If yes, what's it like?

_____

_____

_____

_____

TALK LIKE AN ASTRONAUT!

When astronauts need to say a letter, they use a special **phonetic alphabet** so they won't be misunderstood. The code switches each letter to a whole word. Below see how **Mickey's** name would look in this code. Then write **your** name on the line below using the Code Key.

Mickey = _Mike India Charlie Kilo Echo Yankee_

Your name = _____

CODE KEY

A = Alpha	N = November
B = Bravo	O = Oscar
C = Charlie	P = Papa
D = Delta	Q = Quebec
E = Echo	R = Romeo
F = Foxtrot	S = Sierra
G = Golf	T = Tango
H = Hotel	U = Uniform
I = India	V = Victor
J = Juliet	W = Whiskey
K = Kilo	X = X-ray
L = Lima	Y = Yankee
M = Mike	Z = Zulu

An underwater world surrounds you on Finding Nemo Submarine Voyage.

ADVENTURELAND

What Will You Find in This Land?

ATTRACTIONS
- Enchanted Tiki Room
- Indiana Jones Adventure
- Jungle Cruise
- Tarzan's Treehouse

FOOD & DRINKS
- Aladdin's Oasis
- Bengal Barbecue
- Tiki Juice Bar

SHOPS
- Adventureland Bazaar
- Indiana Jones Adventure Outpost
- South Seas Traders

ALSO IN THIS CHAPTER
- Say Aloha to the Tiki Gods!
- Trash Talk
- Decode the Secret Message!
- The Going To Disneyland Secret Code!
- Unique Souvenirs
- Are You a Numismatist?
- Imagineer Close-up: Rolly Crump

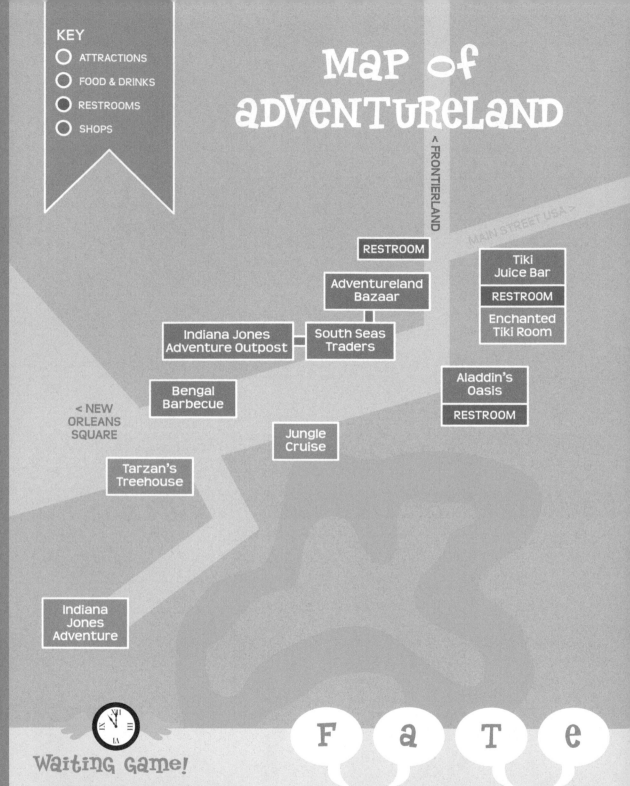

< FRONTIERLAND

MAP of ADVENTURELAND

KEY
- ⚬ ATTRACTIONS
- ⚬ FOOD & DRINKS
- ⬤ RESTROOMS
- ⚬ SHOPS

MAIN STREET USA >

RESTROOM

Adventureland Bazaar

Tiki Juice Bar

RESTROOM

Enchanted Tiki Room

Indiana Jones Adventure Outpost

South Seas Traders

Aladdin's Oasis

RESTROOM

< NEW ORLEANS SQUARE

Bengal Barbecue

Jungle Cruise

Tarzan's Treehouse

Indiana Jones Adventure

F A T E

Waiting Game!

ADVENTURERS' FATE

For this game you need at least 2 players. The object is to spell a word that does NOT end on you. Words that have three letters or fewer don't count. Going in order, one at a time, players say a letter. If you can't think of a letter that will work without spelling a word, you can try to bluff but—beware—the next player can say "I challenge you. What word are you spelling?" If you don't have a real word, you're out. If you do have one, they're out. Each time someone loses a round they get a letter in the word "FATE"—first an F, then an A, then a T, and finally an E. Once someone has gotten out four times and has all the letters, they have met their fate and they lose. The last player standing wins.

> "To create a land that would make this dream reality, we pictured ourselves far from civilization."
> —WALT DISNEY

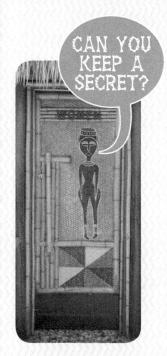

CAN YOU KEEP A SECRET?

Adventurers Welcome

Adventureland mixes the sights and sounds of many different foreign countries, and combines them into one land that's spilling over with bright colors, lush plantlife, exotic patterns and lots and lots of bamboo. As you explore, you'll discover touches of African, Asian, South American, South Pacific and Polynesian tiki culture—all in a vintage 1930-40s setting.

HOT TIP A **LOT** of people crowd into the busy restroom just past the main entrance to Adventureland. Little do they know, there's a "secret" restroom nearby inside the courtyard of **Enchanted Tiki Room!**

FUN FACT

Enchanted Tiki Room was originally going to be a sit-down restaurant with the show going on while people ate.

YUM!

★ Enchanted Tiki Room

INDOOR SHOW — EST. — 1963 — Lively & Exciting

Before you enter this enchanting attraction, enjoy the beautiful tropical courtyard with lush plant life, talking tiki gods and the Tiki Juice Bar, home to one of Disneyland's most beloved treats —the famous pineapple Dole Whip. Once you go inside and take a seat, over 200 talking and singing tropical birds, totem poles, tiki sculptures and flowers around the room come to life and put on a quite a show with songs, jokes, jungle drums and even an electrifying tropical storm!

 HOT TIP If it's not too crowded, ask a **Cast Member** if **YOU** can wake up José to start the show!

Illustration by Scott Corking • www.SideshowDesign.com

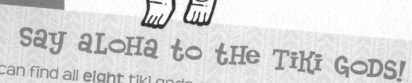

Say aloha to the Tiki Gods!

See if you can find all **eight** tiki gods and godesses in the **courtyard** outside Enchanted Tiki Room. Put a ✓ next to the ones you find below!

- ☐ Hina Kuluua
- ☐ Koro
- ☐ Maui
- ☐ Ngendei
- ☐ Pele
- ☐ Rongo
- ☐ Tangaroa
- ☐ Tangaroa-ru

TIME MACHINE

1933
Tiki culture begins when the first Don the Beachcomber restaurant opens in Hollywood.

1963
Enchanted Tiki Room opens & is the first fully air-conditioned attraction in Disneyland. So cool!

1976
Dole Pineapple Co. starts to host Enchanted Tiki Room & the Tiki Juice Bar, where the Dole Whip was born.

2011
Tiki fans rejoice when the Disneyland Hotel opens Trader Sam's Enchanted Tiki Bar. Kids are allowed in until 8 p.m.

TRASH TALK

Legend has it that Walt Disney got an ice cream bar in Disneyland and ate it as he walked. When he was ready to throw away the stick, he told his staff to make sure that the distance he had just walked was the **longest space** between any two trash cans in the park. In Disneyland, even the trash cans are special. They not only have designs on them, but each one matches the area where it sits. Fans of the park appreciate the cans so much, there are even **trash can-themed souvenirs** like collectible pins and salt shakers!

FUN FACT

When Jungle Cruise first launched, the skippers talked about the scenes in a serious way. It wasn't until the 1960s that the ride was changed to have funny scenes & jokes!

HA HA!

★ Jungle Cruise

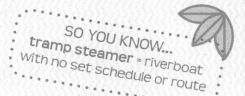

SO YOU KNOW... **tramp steamer** = riverboat with no set schedule or route

Wind through the River Expedition Company's 1930s-style boathouse to climb aboard a **tramp steamer**. Sit back and relax as your friendly, funny Skipper tells you all about the sights to see including a waterfall, wild animals, explorers and even headhunters! The comical cruise takes you through the tropical jungle rivers of Asia, Africa and South America before you experience what many call the most dangerous part of your journey —the return to civilization!

OUTDOOR BOAT RIDE ★ Lively & Exciting ★ est. 1955

HOT TIP There are sometimes **free** Jungle Cruise maps. After you exit your boat, ask a Cast Member if they are being handed out that day.

SPY Each of the Jungle Cruise boats has a name. Fill in the **name** of the boat you ride on and circle the **month** and **date** of your trip on the ticket below:

JAN FEB MAR APR MAY JUN JUL AUG SEP OCT NOV DEC

1 2 3 4 5 6 7 8 9 10 11 12 13 14 15 16 17

JUNGLE CRUISE
SPECIAL EXCURSION
Round Trip Ticket

BOAT NAME _____

TOURS DEPARTING DAILY

18 19 20 21 22 23 24 25 26 27 28 29 30 31

CONGO QUEEN

Illustration by Steve White

TIME MACHINE

1948
Disney's True-Life Adventure movies later inspire a jungle boat ride for Disneyland.

1954
Work on Jungle Cruise starts first, so that the plants have more time to grow.

1955
Jungle Cruise is an Opening Day attraction in Disneyland & is the only Adventureland attraction for seven years!

2013
An annual tradition begins when Jungle Cruise becomes Jingle Cruise for the holidays. Jingle all the way!

★ Tarzan's Treehouse

★ OUTDOOR WALK-THROUGH ★ CALM & MELLOW ★ est. 1999

Walk through the story of Tarzan as you climb the 80-foot tree he calls home. You'll see cozy rooms built into the tree filled with **curiosities** salvaged from the ship that brought him to the African rainforest. As you explore, look for the pages of Jane's **sketchbook** to tell you more about Tarzan's exciting adventures. Before you climb back down, be sure to take a moment to check out the **amazing view** from up here!

HOT TIP
Don't rush past the snarling leopard, **Sabor,** up in the tree. If she isn't doing anything, give her a few minutes but be ready for a **surprise!**

SPY
The **Base Camp** at the foot of the treehouse is full of fun stuff to check out. See if you can spot **Mrs. Potts and Chip** from *Beauty and the Beast.*

FUN FACT

The *"Swisskapolka"* music used to play on a gramophone in Swiss Family Treehouse. As a nod to the old attraction, a gramophone in Tarzan's Treehouse plays the same song.

SOUNDS GOOD!

"Now, you stay away from me. Like a very good wild man."
—JANE PORTER

TIME MACHINE

1960
Disney releases the movie "Swiss Family Robinson," based on a book by Johann David Wyss from 1812.

1962
Swiss Family Treehouse opens in Disneyland. Charming!

1999
Disney releases the animated movie "Tarzan," based on a book by Edgar Rice Burroughs from 1912.

1999
The treehouse gets a new entrance over a rope bridge & a new theme when it becomes Tarzan's Treehouse.

FUN FACT

Between Jungle Cruise & Indiana Jones Adventure sits the Dominguez tree. When the Dominguez family sold the land to Walt Disney to make Disneyland, they asked that the palm tree— which had been planted in 1896 as a wedding gift—be saved.

SWEET!

★ Indiana Jones Adventure

INDOOR DARK RIDE ★ -est.- 1995 ★ WILD & THRILLING

MAY BE SCARY !

Strap yourself in to a rugged transport truck for a **rip-roaring** ride through the cursed Temple of the Forbidden Eye. There you'll encounter the god **Mara**. This ancient god grants eternal youth, earthly riches or knowledge of the future to those **pure of heart** and **DOOM** to those foolish enough to gaze into its eyes. You'll face treacherous cliffs, molten lava, slithering snakes, swarms of insects and an enormous boulder headed **straight for your truck!** This ride has a special computer that changes things up each time, making thousands of possible **adventures** so you'll never know just what might happen next.

 HOT TIP Can't get enough Indiana Jones? Head to **Indiana Jones Adventure Outpost** to try out a cool, custom Indiana Jones **pinball machine!**

 SPY There's **LOTS** to look at in the line for this ride, like real movie props and intriguing signs like one that says: "Do not pull rope!" **But go ahead and pull it!**

Mini Quiz!

Can you guess which one of these things Indiana Jones hates most of all?
Answer on page 181.
☐ Rats   ☐ Snakes   ☐ Spiders

TIME MACHINE

1930
Action heroes in movie serials of this decade later inspire filmmaker George Lucas—the creator of "Star Wars."

1973
George Lucas writes "The Adventures of Indiana Smith." Steven Spielberg suggests he change the name to Jones.

1981
"Raiders of the Lost Ark," directed by Steven Spielberg, is the first in the Indiana Jones movie series.

1995
Indiana Jones Adventure opens in Disneyland. Da-da-da-da!

DeCoDe tHe SeCReT MeSSaGe!

Indiana Jones wants you to **watch out** for something inside the Temple. Use the **code key** on **page 118** to decipher his message. If you ride **Indiana Jones Adventure**, see if you can spot this during the ride!

Answer on page 181.

THE GOING TO DISNEYLAND SECRET CODE!

Adventurers sometimes have to decipher messages written in **secret codes.** This code turns **each letter** of the alphabet into a symbol of something found in Disneyland that starts with that **same letter.** Write your name or your own secret message on the scrap of paper below!

Code Key

A Apple	B Balloon	C Castle	D Dwarf	E Ears	F Fireworks	G Ghost

H Hook	I Ice Cream	J Jewel	K Knight	L Lollipop	M Matterhorn	N Nemo

O Olaf	P Peter Pan	Q Queen	R Rocket	S Snow White	T Teacup	U Umbrella

V Vehicle	W Winnie	X X marks the spot	Y Yoda	Z Zebra

"If you are what you eat then I
only want to eat the good stuff."
—REMY

★ Food & Drinks

ALADDIN'S OASIS

An oasis is a green spot in the desert with plants and water—a little area of relief from the harsh elements. This oasis, named after Princess Jasmine's main man, serves on-the-go meals to take out or enjoy at the tables on their pretty patio.

- *Grilled chicken*
- *Lasagna*
- *Mac n' cheese*

FUN FACT

The Tiki Juice Bar sometimes has fun, FREE souvenirs like buttons that say "First Dole Whip" & cute cards with a tiki on one side & a recipe that uses pineapple on the other.

NICE!

BENGAL BARBECUE

This walk-up food stand is named after Bengal tigers like Shere Khan from *The Jungle Book*.

- *Meat or veggie skewers*
- *Tiger Tails breadsticks*

TIKI JUICE BAR

Do you love pineapples? Then this is the place for you! Serving up tasty pineapple treats, the Tiki Juice Bar is located at the entrance of Enchanted Tiki Room.

- *Dole Whip float* • *Pineapple Dole Whip soft-serve*

 HOT TIP Many people don't realize you can visit the Tiki Juice Bar from **inside** the courtyard so, the line inside is often **shorter**!

★ Unique Souvenirs

WiTCH DOCTOR PRESCRIPTION

Hanging around in **South Seas Traders** is a shrunken head called Shrunken Ned, the Jungle Witch Doctor. Pop two quarters in the slot, place your hand on the handprint and Colonel Nedley Lotsmore will give you his friendly advice and a funny fortune card.

> SO YOU KNOW...
> **Rajah** = king or prince in India

SMUSHED Penny

The elephant on top of **Rajah's** Mint Penny Press in **Adventureland Bazaar** stamps your penny into a whole new shape and design while you wait and then comes out warm—literally "hot off the press."

Illustrations by Scott Cocking • www.SideShowDesign.com

aRE you a numismatist?

If you collect pressed coins like the ones from Rajah's Mint, YOU are a **"NOO-MIZ-MUH-TIST"**—someone who studies or collects **coins.** Pressed coins became a popular souvenir in America in 1893 during the **Chicago World's Fair,** where people chose from four designs celebrating Christoper Columbus. Today in the Disneyland Resort, there are **hundreds** of unique designs to choose from at machines that press not just pennies but nickels, dimes and quarters too. Want to collect them all? Head to **City Hall** and pick up a free **Pressed Coin Location Guide.**

 Pennies made after 1982 have a **zinc core** and may create a pressed penny with silver streaks!

 Look out for a special coin press machine in **Mickey's Toontown.** It's the only one in the park that presses **dimes.**

IMAGINEER CLOSE-UP: ROLLY CRUMP

Rolly Crump's story really shows you how one little thing can lead to something **BIG!** Rolly was working as a lowly peon in Disney's animation department when Walt Disney saw some **propellers** and **mobiles** Rolly had made in his free time. Walt was impressed and offered Rolly a new job as one of the first Imagineers! Today you can see Rolly's work all over Disneyland. He designed the charming **It's a Small World** clock tower, the incredible **Enchanted Tiki Room** sculptures, the exotic **Adventureland Bazaar** and more! Sometimes Imagineers' projects don't actually get made. One of the most legendary "Attractions That Never Were" is Rolly's **Museum of the Weird**—a walk-through exhibit of wonderfully strange curiosities for Haunted Mansion. Walt loved the early ideas for the museum but, sadly, he passed away in the middle of the Haunted Mansion project. Without his support, the plans for the museum were **cancelled.** The bright side is that many of Rolly's ideas were still used in the **final version** of the attraction. The most amazing thing about Rolly Crump is that he never had any **formal art training.** He dove into every project head first and learned whatever he needed to as he went along to get the job done—**in style!**

CLOCKWISE FROM TOP LEFT:
- Caricature Rolly Crump drew of himself for this book—thanks Rolly!
- Tiki god Maui fills a bamboo pole with water outside Enchanted Tiki Room
- Rolly's spooky sketch of a man-eating plant for the Museum of the Weird
- The famous Haunted Mansion wallpaper that developed from Rolly's man-eating plant sketch
- Doors open, dolls dance and whirligigs whirl on It's a Small World's joyful clock tower

Exotic tiki carvings and skulls decorate the wooden bridge from Main Street USA to Adventureland.

FRONTIERLAND

What Will You Find in This Land?

ENTERTAINMENT
- Fantasmic!
- Farley the Fiddler
- The Laughing Stock Co.
- Mariachi Music

ATTRACTIONS
- Big Thunder Mountain Railroad
- Mark Twain Riverboat
- Pirate's Lair on Tom Sawyer Island
- Sailing Ship Columbia

FOOD & DRINKS
- The Golden Horseshoe
- Rancho del Zocalo Restaurante
- River Belle Terrace
- Stage Door Café

SHOPS
- Bonanza Outfitters
- Leather Shop
- Pioneer Mercantile
- Westward Ho Trading Co.

ALSO IN THIS CHAPTER
- Wild West Explorers' Quest!
- The Rivers of America
- ¡Buen Apetito!
- Unique Souvenirs
- Ready, Aim, Fire
- The Halloween Tree
- The Petrified Tree
- Imagineer Close-up: Bill Evans

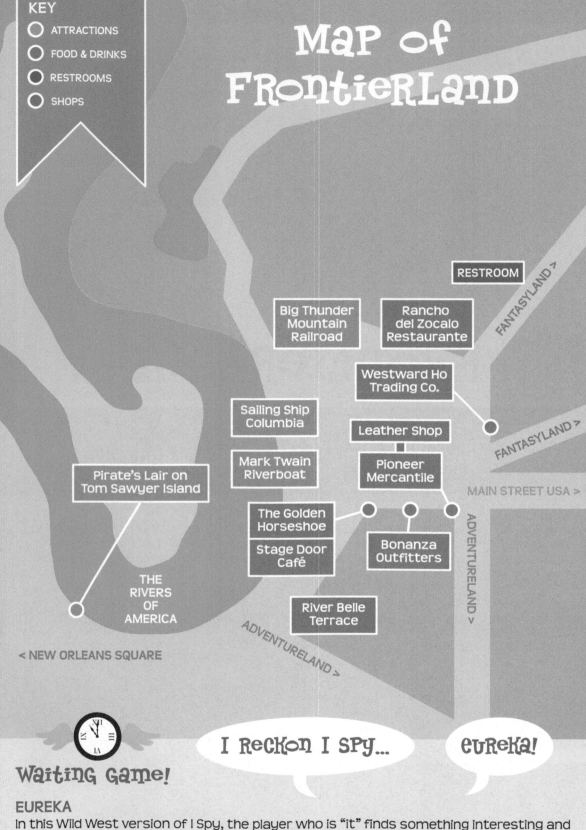

MAP of FRONtieRLaND

KEY
- ○ ATTRACTIONS
- ○ FOOD & DRINKS
- ● RESTROOMS
- ○ SHOPS

RESTROOM

FANTASYLAND >

Big Thunder Mountain Railroad

Rancho del Zocalo Restaurante

Westward Ho Trading Co.

FANTASYLAND >

Sailing Ship Columbia

Leather Shop

Mark Twain Riverboat

Pioneer Mercantile

MAIN STREET USA >

Pirate's Lair on Tom Sawyer Island

The Golden Horseshoe

Stage Door Café

Bonanza Outfitters

ADVENTURELAND >

THE RIVERS OF AMERICA

River Belle Terrace

< NEW ORLEANS SQUARE

ADVENTURELAND >

I RecKon I Spy...

eureKa!

WaitiNG Game!

EUREKA
In this Wild West version of I Spy, the player who is "it" finds something interesting and says, for example, "I reckon I spy an American flag over yonder." The first person to spot the object, point it out and say "Eureka!" is the winner. "Eureka" is actually the California state motto and means "I have found it" in Greek. Each state has a motto—a word or phrase that represents what they're all about—and California's is related to the discovery of gold in the state. **NOTE:** When you are it, try to spy something that's not on the move so that the other players have time to try and find it!

Hey Howdy Hey

Stroll down wooden boardwalks, past prickly desert cactus and towering rock pillars, as you explore the wild, wild Western style of Frontierland. This land is a mix of cowboy, Native American Indian and Mexican themes, and sits on the bustling waterfront of the Rivers of America. In the 1800s, daring American trailblazers explored the unknown frontiers of the western United States. When settlers discovered that there was *"gold in them thar hills"* in 1848, Gold Fever swept the nation and the California Gold Rush began. Tens of thousands of pioneers went west to strike it rich, and towns and forts sprung up all over that looked just like Frontierland.

★ Entertainment

For showtimes, pick up an Entertainment Times Guide at the Main Entrance, get info at City Hall or ask a friendly Cast Member.

- **Fantasmic!**—Mickey Mouse stars in an outdoor nighttime show in the waterfront area with projected images, lasers and other special effects
- **Farley the Fiddler**—strolling violin player
- **The Laughing Stock Co.**—songs and jokes in The Golden Horseshoe
- **Mariachi Music**—strolling traditional Mexican folk musicians

FUN FACT

Mark Twain was a famous author & humorist, but he never even finished elementary school!

WHAT?!

"Give every day the chance to become the most beautiful day of your life."
—MARK TWAIN

★ Mark Twain Riverboat

OUTDOOR Boat Ride ★ est. 1955 ★ CALM & MELLOW

Travel in style aboard a steam-powered riverboat as it paddles around Tom Sawyer Island on the Rivers of America. This beautiful boat is a working reproduction of the 19th-century riverboats that carried people and cargo along America's rivers and has a real, working steam engine that makes it go. While on board, check out the **Promenade** Deck, the Texas Deck, the Main Deck and the Pilothouse, where the Captain's Quarters and Wheelhouse are located. As you enjoy the ride, listen up for narration about the interesting sights to see as you enjoy your cruise.

HOT TIP Ask a Cast Member if you can ride in the **Wheelhouse**. They might even let you pull the **whistle** and ring the **bell**!

SO YOU KNOW... promenade = area used for slow strolls

TIME MACHINE

1835
Samuel L. Clemens is born & later changes his name to Mark Twain, the term for water that's 2 fathoms deep & safe for boats.

1859
Mark Twain gets his steamboat pilot's license & works on the Mississippi River.

1876
Mark Twain becomes famous for his book "The Adventures of Tom Sawyer."

1955
Mark Twain Riverboat launches in Disneyland as an Opening Day attraction. By the mark!

Sailing Ship Columbia

Set sail for adventure as you climb aboard this majestic **replica** of an 18th-century sailing ship. This seaworthy **vessel** is 110-feet long with an 84-foot tall mainmast. The two deck-mounted guns and ten cannons would be perfect for fighting off the **dastardly pirates** that terrorized ships like this back in the Golden Age of Piracy. Enjoy the ride up top or head below deck to the **Crew Quarters** to enjoy maritime displays showing what life was like for the sailors on the **original** Columbia Rediviva ship.

Outdoor Boat Ride ★ *Calm & Mellow* — est. **1958**

 HOT TIP
Sailing Ship Columbia follows the same route as **Mark Twain Riverboat**.

 SPY
Keep your eyes peeled for **Sailing Ship Columbia** and **Mark Twain Riverboat** making special appearances in the nighttime show **Fantasmic!**

FUN FACT

Shipbuilders have a custom of placing a silver dollar under each mast for good luck. When Walt Disney learned this, he made sure to be there the day the masts were added so he could put the silver dollars in place himself.

LUCKY!

"Riches don't make a man rich, they only make him busier."
—CHRISTOPHER COLUMBUS

TIME MACHINE

1773
The original Columbia ship is built & named after Christopher Columbus, who sailed the ocean blue in 1492.

1787
The Columbia is rebuilt & named Columbia Rediviva—a Latin word that means returned to life or revived.

1790
The Columbia Rediviva is the first American ship to circle the globe.

1958
Ahoy, sailors! Disneyland's replica of the Columbia Rediviva welcomes its first passengers aboard.

★ Big Thunder Mountain Railroad

ROLLER COASTER · est. · 1979 · WILD & THRILLING

Hang on to them hats n' glasses, 'cause this here's the wildest ride in the wilderness! Hop aboard a **runaway mine train** and hurtle back to the days of the Gold Rush. As the train speeds into a **dark cavern,** you'll see screeching bats and rainbow-colored pools of water. Back outside, you'll dip and dive over hills and spiral past a **hungry goat.** Warning signs are everywhere as the train enters an abandoned mine shaft but it's **too late** to turn back now. After an **explosive** exit, you'll wind past the rustic mining town of Rainbow Ridge and live to tell the tale of your **wild, western** adventure.

SPY Look for a **funny name** on the side of the train. Will you ride the I.B. Hearty, I.M. Fearless, I.M. Loco, U.B. Bold, U.R. Courageous or U.R. Daring? Write the name of the train you ride in on the side of the train below:

BIG THUNDER MOUNTAIN RR

FUN FACT

The unusual rock formations you see on Big Thunder Mountain Railroad are made to look like the towering rock pillars in Utah's Bryce Canyon called "Hoodoos."

HOO KNEW?

TIME MACHINE

1956	1960	1979	2014
Rainbow Caverns Mine Train chugs slowly through Frontierland. Woot! Woot!	*The train ride changes to Mine Train Through Nature's Wonderland but closes in 1977 for Big Thunder Mountain.*	*Big Thunder Mountain Railroad's high-speed runaway trains dash through Frontierland for the first time.*	*Big Thunder Mountain Railroad gets an upgrade with a new track & new special effects.*

Model of Big Thunder Mountain Railroad by 16-year-old Disneyland fan, Kolby Ratigan!

WiLD WeST eXPLOReRS' QueST!

YEEHAW!

Pioneers explore new lands and make **amazing discoveries** along the way. Say **"Yeehaw!"** when you spot these sights in Frontierland and **conquer** this wild frontier! Put a ✓ next to the ones you find.

- ☐ Silhouette of a Mexican vaquero cowboy on the Rancho del Zocalo sign
- ☐ Native American Indian statue near Westward Ho Trading Co.
- ☐ Horseshoe prints and wagon wheel marks on the ground
- ☐ Golden horseshoe on the sign for The Golden Horseshoe
- ☐ Owl in a dead tree at Frontierland Shootin' Exposition
- ☐ Flags flying on the fort entrance to Frontierland

FUN FaCT

Disneyland Guests used to enjoy fishing off the docks of Tom Sawyer Island.

"REEL FUN!"

MAY BE SCARY
⚠

Pirate's Lair on Tom Sawyer Island

OUTDOOR PLAY AReA
-est.- 2007
Lively & exciting

Log rafts will carry you across the scenic **Rivers of America** to this rough and tumble island named after the main character in **Mark Twain's** most famous book, *The Adventures of Tom Sawyer.* You'll feel just like a pirate when you **explore** the dark tunnels, swaying rope bridges and curving paths that snake around the island. Scurry over to **Smuggler's Cove** for interactive pirate-themed fun, peek into telescopes on **Castle Rock** to spy on the mainland, and sit your booty on piles of pirate booty at the **Captain's Treasure.** If you're feeling really daring, enter the **Dead Man's Grotto**—a spooky cave where you just might find the chest of Davy Jones!

👁 **SPY** Keep a weather eye open, there are *Pirates of the Caribbean* touches all over the island —like Will Turner's blacksmith shop.

TIME MACHINE

1650	1876	1956	2007
Pirates terrorize the seas during the Golden Age of Piracy until around the year 1730. Arrrrgh!	*Mark Twain writes "The Adventures of Tom Sawyer."*	*Tom Sawyer Island welcomes its first explorers.*	*After the success of the "Pirates of the Caribbean" movies, the Pirate's Lair is added to Tom Sawyer island.*

THE RIVERS of AMERICA

Map of TOM SAWYER ISLAND

UNCHARTED LANDS

FORT WILDERNESS

CAPTAIN'S TREASURE

SHIPWRECK

PONTOON BRIDGE

SMUGGLER'S COVE

CASTLE ROCK

SUSPENSION BRIDGE

TOM & HUCK'S TREEHOUSE

RESTROOM

DEAD MAN'S GROTTO

W. TURNER BLACKSMITH

LAFITTE'S TAVERN

THE RIVERS OF AMERICA

BOARD RAFTS HERE

Tom Sawyer Island is in the middle of a body of water called **the Rivers of America.** Water birds have flown in and made their home here along with carp, salmon, catfish and turtles. But there are some **odd things** in the river too. The story goes that when the river was drained for maintenance work, Cast Members found hundreds of cell phones, a fake leg and **half of a canoe!** There are **four ways** to travel on the Rivers of America (see note below). If you ride on the river, keep your eyes peeled for many interesting animals and scenes along the riverbanks. You never know what you might see!

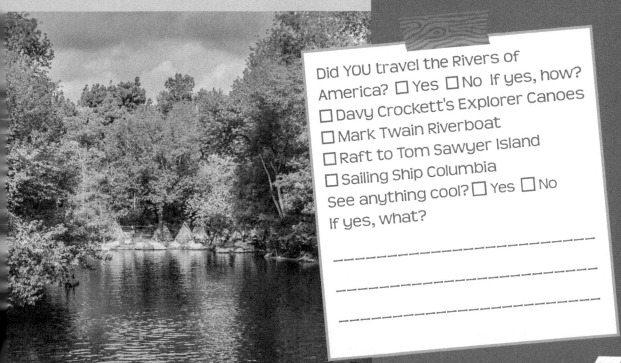

Did YOU travel the Rivers of America? ☐ Yes ☐ No If yes, how?
☐ Davy Crockett's Explorer Canoes
☐ Mark Twain Riverboat
☐ Raft to Tom Sawyer Island
☐ Sailing Ship Columbia
See anything cool? ☐ Yes ☐ No
If yes, what?

_____
_____
_____

FUN FACT
Imagineer Harper Goff designed The Golden Horseshoe to look like the horseshoe-shaped theater he created for the 1953 Doris Day musical "Calamity Jane."

GOSH ALMIGHTY!

★ # Food & Drinks

THE GOLDEN HORSESHOE

The Golden Horseshoe is an old-timey saloon like you'd have found in the days of the Old West. Check the schedule to catch a live show while ya enjoy yer grub. In a rush? Mosey around back to the quick service window at **Stage Door Café.**

• *Chicken nuggets* • *Chili* • *Fish & chips* • *Root beer floats*

HOT TIP — See if you can sit in Walt and Lillian Disney's **box seats**, now open to the public, upstairs to the right of the stage.

RIVER BELLE TERRACE

This elegant restaurant full of southern charm offers dining inside, or outside under tasseled umbrellas.

• *French toast* • *Mickey pancakes* • *Sandwiches* • *Salads*

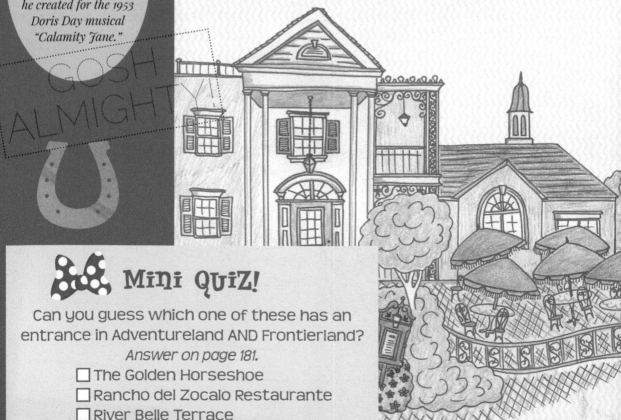

MINI QUIZ!

Can you guess which one of these has an entrance in Adventureland AND Frontierland?
Answer on page 181.
☐ The Golden Horseshoe
☐ Rancho del Zocalo Restaurante
☐ River Belle Terrace

Rancho Del Zocalo Restaurante

This Mexican restaurant has an indoor dining room with glowing star-shaped lanterns and a lovely, flower-filled shady patio.

• Burritos • Salads • Soup • Tacos

 Choose a table right next to the wall that separates **Rancho Del Zocalo Restaurante** from Big Thunder Mountain Railroad to watch the **train cars** speed by while you eat!

SO YOU KNOW...
Rancho del Zocalo =
Ranch of the town square

¡Buen Apetito! (Enjoy Your Meal)

Not sure what some of the Mexican items are on the menu at **Rancho del Zocalo Restaurante**? Here's the rundown on some of the things you can choose from. Which one sounds the most **"delicioso"** to you?

☀ Arroz con Frijoles/Pollo
Arroz = Rice
Con = With
Frijoles = Beans
Pollo = Chicken

☀ Burrito
Meat and/or bean-filled flour tortilla folded in cylinder shape

☀ Carne Asada
Marinated steak cooked with a charred or lightly burnt flavor

☀ Enchilada
Chili pepper sauce covering a meat- or cheese-filled folded corn tortilla

☀ Flan
Round pudding-like cake coated with sweet syrup

☀ Pollo en Mole
Chicken with spicy chocolate and peanut sauce

☀ Tortilla
Thin flatbread made from corn or flour

☀ Tostada
Fried tortilla—Tostada means "fried"

☀ Tres Leches Cake
A sponge cake soaked in 3 kinds of milk: evaporated milk, condensed milk and heavy cream. Leches = Milk

★ Unique Souvenirs

COONSKIN CAP

Pioneer Mercantile is the place to pick up your very own imitation racoon hat just like Fess Parker wore when he played Davy Crockett in the wildly popular 1950's Disney TV series.

Illustration by Steve Willis

CUSTOMIZED LEATHER

Choose from bracelets, belts, keychains and more, and watch as Cast Members stamp it with your name or message at the **Leather Shop** in front of Pioneer Mercantile.

READY, AIM, FIRE

Right beside Westward Ho Trading Co. is **Frontierland Shootin' Exposition.** Sidle up to the counter of this shooting gallery, slide your change in the slot and aim your rifle at moving and still **targets.** If you hit the mark, the object you hit will light up, make a sound or move—and sometimes **it'll do all three!** There are almost a **hundred** targets to shoot at like tombstones, cactus, a moving train, a digging shovel and a dead tree. Best of all? It only costs **fifty cents!**

HOT TIP Real cowboys and cowgirls didn't have such high-tech rifles. The guns at **Frontierland Shootin' Exposition** actually fire invisible beams of infrared light!

SO YOU KNOW...
exposition =
public exhibit or show

THe HaLLoween TRee

If you happen to be in Disneyland during the **Halloween** season—which usually starts in early September—be sure to visit this **oak tree** near The Golden Horseshoe. Decked out in **festive lights** and **painted pumpkins**, the tree is a tribute to author Ray Bradbury's book *The Halloween Tree.* Bradbury was friends with Walt Disney and a fan of Disneyland.

THe PeTRiFieD TRee

This **55-million-year-old** tree is so old it has actually turned to **stone!** The story goes that Walt Disney bought it for his wife as an **Anniversary gift** but she joked it was "too large for the mantle" above their fireplace and presented it to **Disneyland.**

ImaGineeR CLoSe–UP: BiLL eVans

Disneyland's incredibly beautiful **landscaping** was created by Disney Legend **Morgan "Bill" Evans.** He had done some gardening work at Walt Disney's home and Walt liked it so much that he asked him to plan the **plant life** for Disneyland too. The budget was tight so Bill got creative. He scored **free trees** that were being removed to build a freeway nearby and planted trees **upside down** on the banks of the Jungle Cruise river because the twisty-turny roots looked like exotic **tropical branches.** When a **Dawn Redwood** tree that was thought to be extinct was discovered in China in 1941, Bill was given one of only four samples—and he planted it in Disneyland!

SPY

You can still see the special **Dawn Redwood tree** today between **The Golden Horseshoe** and **Stage Door Café.**

While on Big Thunder Mountain Railroad, you'll whizz past the mining town of Rainbow Ridge.

NEW ORLEANS SQUARE

What Will You Find in This Land?

ENTERTAINMENT
- The Bootstrappers
- Jambalaya Jazz Band
- Royal Street Bachelors

ATTRACTIONS
- Disneyland Railroad
- Haunted Mansion
- Pirates of the Caribbean

FOOD & DRINKS
- Blue Bayou Restaurant
- Café Orleans
- French Market Restaurant
- Mint Julep Bar
- Royal Street Veranda

SHOPS
- Le Bat en Rouge
- Cristal d'Orleans
- La Mascarade d'Orleans
- Mlle. Antoinette's Parfumerie
- Parasol Cart
- Pieces of Eight
- Port Royal

ALSO IN THIS CHAPTER
- Pirate-ize These Pix!
- Imagineer Close-up: X Atencio
- Secret Spots
- Bon Appétit!
- Unique Souvenirs
- Anchors Away
- Vicious Villains!

MAP of New ORLeans Square

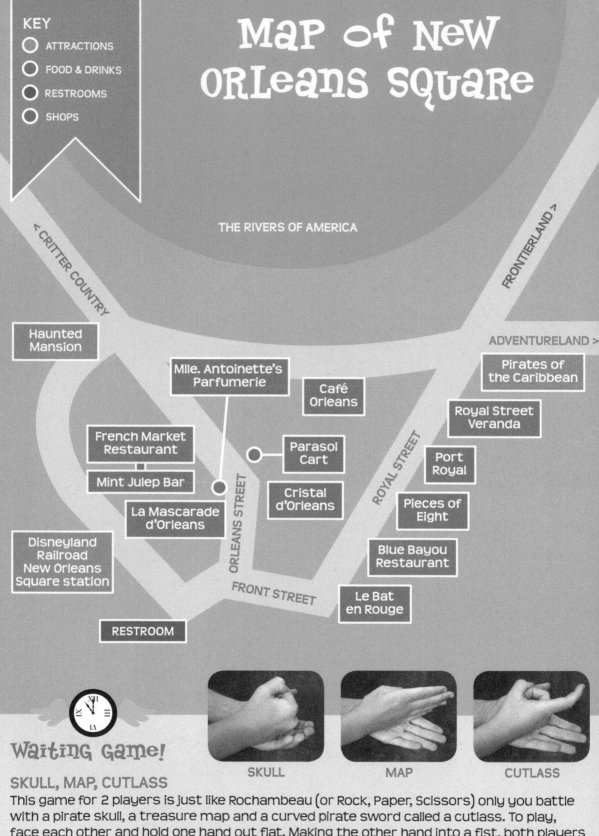

KEY
- ○ ATTRACTIONS
- ○ FOOD & DRINKS
- ● RESTROOMS
- ○ SHOPS

< CRITTER COUNTRY

FRONTIERLAND >

THE RIVERS OF AMERICA

ADVENTURELAND >

Haunted Mansion

Mlle. Antoinette's Parfumerie

Café Orleans

Pirates of the Caribbean

Royal Street Veranda

French Market Restaurant

Parasol Cart

Port Royal

Mint Julep Bar

Cristal d'Orleans

Pieces of Eight

La Mascarade d'Orleans

ORLEANS STREET

ROYAL STREET

Disneyland Railroad New Orleans Square station

Blue Bayou Restaurant

FRONT STREET

Le Bat en Rouge

RESTROOM

SKULL

MAP

CUTLASS

Waiting Game!

SKULL, MAP, CUTLASS

This game for 2 players is just like Rochambeau (or Rock, Paper, Scissors) only you battle with a pirate skull, a treasure map and a curved pirate sword called a cutlass. To play, face each other and hold one hand out flat. Making the other hand into a fist, both players tap their fist onto the palm of their hands for three counts, in the same rhythm. On the fourth count, each player shows a skull (keep hand in a fist), a map (straight hand), or a cutlass (one curved finger). The skull crushes the cutlass, the cutlass slices the map and the map smothers the skull.

Let the Good Times Roll

New Orleans Square looks an awful lot like a part of the real city of New Orleans, Louisiana called the French Quarter. It's one of the few areas in Disneyland that was made to look like an actual place, with winding side alleys and two-story buildings with tall shuttered windows and ornate metal balconies spilling over with plants and flowers. New Orleans—and New Orleans Square—is known for its unique southern food, exciting live music and its wild, colorful Mardi Gras celebrations.

★ Entertainment

For showtimes, pick up an Entertainment Times Guide at the Main Entrance, get info at City Hall or ask a friendly Cast Member.

- **The Bootstrappers**—roving band of merry pirate musicians
- **Jambalaya Jazz Band**—New Orleans-style jazz band
- **Royal Street Bachelors**—traditional jazz and blues band
  NOTE: Both jazz bands perform at French Market Restaurant and various other spots around New Orleans Square.

RATE THIS ATTRACTION

- ☐ Never. Again.
- ☐ Not so hot.
- ☐ Pretty cool...
- ☐ Way cool!
- ☐ Awesome!!
- ☐ AHH, MY FAVE!!!

One word I'd use to describe this attraction:

_____

FUN FACT

To make New Orleans Square feel like a real port, Imagineers added the mast & sail of a ship in the distance. To spot this illusion, stand in front of Pirates of the Caribbean near the Rivers of America & look to the right over the rooftops of New Orleans Square.

AHOY!

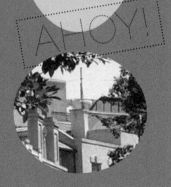

⭐ Pirates of the Caribbean

INDOOR Boat Ride ★ est. 1967 ★ Lively & exciting

Arrrrrrrr ye ready for a swashbuckling adventure? Your journey begins as you board a boat and cruise through a peaceful evening on the **bayou**. A talking skull warns you of danger ahead right before your boat plummets into darkness and splashes down into the pirate-infested waters of the Caribbean! You'll hear strains of the classic song *Yo Ho (A Pirate's Life for Me)* and a distant voice chanting "Dead men tell no tales" as you float through an underground grotto past the skeletons of doomed pirates. Rounding a dark corner, flashes of lightning illuminate a spooky shipwreck and mounds of glittering treasure dazzle in the Captain's Quarters. As you enter a foggy harbor, guns and cannons blast in a fierce battle between a pirate galleon and an island fort. Up ahead, pirates are running wild, ransacking a town and even catching it on fire. With the town burning around you, your boat will head uphill to go back to the bayou.

HOT TIP
Rumor has it that all the skeletons in this ride are fake **except** for the skull on the headboard of the **Captain's bed!**

SPY
See how many times you can spot **Captain Jack Sparrow** from the *Pirates of the Caribbean* movie series in this ride.

TIME MACHINE

1967
Pirates of the Caribbean & Blue Bayou Restaurant open the year after the rest of New Orleans Square.

2003
The first "Pirates of the Caribbean" movie is inspired by Disneyland's ride & features Captain Jack Sparrow.

2006
Avast, mateys! Characters from the popular "Pirates of the Caribbean" movie series are added to the ride.

2007
"Pirates of the Caribbean" fever takes over Tom Sawyer Island when Pirate's Lair is added.

Pirate-ize These Pix!

Ariel, Cinderella, Tarzan and Kristoff are going to ride Pirates of the Caribbean. Get a pen and turn them into **pirates** by adding "pirate-y" details like those you see here. The first one's been done for you.

MAY BE SCARY

⭐ Haunted Mansion

INDOOR DARK RIDE ★ —est.— 1969 ★ lively & exciting

Look alive! After you enter the dimly lit foyer of the mansion, you'll be ushered to the **dead center** of a small room where the eerie voice of your **Ghost Host** asks, "Is this haunted room actually stretching?" If you can find a way out, you'll walk past a series of changing **portraits** and a pair of staring **statues** —whose sinister eyes seem to follow you wherever you go! After hopping into a **Doom Buggy**, you'll glide past an endless hallway with a floating candelabra, doors that breathe and moan, and the famous **demon eye wallpaper.** In the Seance Room, a floating crystal ball with the head of Madame Leota inside will ask spirits for **a message from somewhere beyond**, before you move to a magnificent ballroom where luminous ghosts dance, dine and duel with pistols. Next, it's on to the attic where a sinister bride pledges **'til death do us part** to a string of unlucky husbands as the Hatbox Ghost looks on. The grand finale is a graveyard full of **happy haunts** who've come out to socialize!

FUN FACT

Haunted Mansion's "Grim Grinning Ghosts" song includes singing by Thurl Ravenscroft. He's also famous for singing "You're a Mean One, Mr. Grinch" in "How the Grinch Stole Christmas!" & for being the voice of Tony the Tiger.

GRRREAT!

HOT TIP

Scoot over! Before you exit this ride, you'll pass three **Hitchhiking Ghosts**—Phineas, Ezra and Gus—and one of them will catch a ride with you!

SPY

As you glide up the exit ramp, watch for one last spirit, **Little Leota.** Madame Leota in the Seance Room and this ghost are dead ringers for **Imagineer Leota Toombs.**

TIME MACHINE

1969	2001	2003	2015
Six years after the outside is built, Haunted Mansion opens with 999 happy haunts—but there's always room for one more.	*The annual "Haunted Mansion Holiday" theme begins with "The Nightmare Before Christmas" decorations.*	*The movie "The Haunted Mansion" based on the ride hits theaters. BOO!*	*Forty-six years after the Hatbox Ghost disappears from the ride, he returns to celebrate Disneyland's 60th Anniversary.*

"We'll take care of the outside and the ghosts will take care of the inside."
—WALT DISNEY

SPY See if you can find **this lady** inside Haunted Mansion! **NOTE:** She won't have a Mint Julep or an alligator purse and her umbrella will be open.

Disneyland Railroad

New Orleans Square is one of the four stops on the Disneyland Railroad.
More info on page 44.

More info on page 44.

MICKEY'S TOONTOWN

NEW ORLEANS SQUARE

TOMORROWLAND

MAIN STREET USA

FUN FACT

At the New Orleans Square train station, you can hear the sound of a telegraph machine tapping out a pattern of sounds in Morse code. So, what's the message saying? It's part of Walt Disney's speech from Disneyland's Opening Day.

COOL!

Illustration by Lindsay Gibson • www.etsy.com/shop/emandsprout

IMAGINEER CLOSE-UP: X ATENCIO

Francis Xavier Atencio, known as **X Atencio**, was working as a Disney Imagineer when Walt Disney asked him to write the ride script and song lyrics for two attractions—**Haunted Mansion** and **Pirates of the Caribbean.** X had never written before but gave it a try and created two of the park's most beloved songs *Grim Grinning Ghosts* and *Yo Ho (A Pirate's Life for Me).* X also wrote the **clever tombstones** you see near the entrance to Haunted Mansion which are actually tributes to his fellow Imagineers. Listen carefully in Haunted Mansion and you can hear X's voice saying **"Hey! Let me out of here!"** as a corpse tries to escape from a coffin. His voice is also the one you hear if the attraction temporarily stops saying **"Playful spooks have interrupted our tour..."** On Pirates of the Caribbean, it's X's voice coming out of the talking skull you see overhead warning you **"It be too late to alter course, mateys."**

Secret Spots

New Orleans Square is home to two fancy-schmancy, exclusive experiences—the **Disneyland Dream Suite** and **Club 33.**

Can you imagine spending the night in Disneyland? People do! Look up the grand, sweeping staircase over Pirates of the Caribbean and you'll see the location of a special hotel room called the **Disneyland Dream Suite.** This spacious apartment includes a **New Orleans -themed living room,** a firefly-filled patio, a private balcony looking over the Rivers of America, an **Adventureland-themed bedroom** and a **Frontierland-themed bedroom.** The suite is filled with special lighting and sound effects, and unusual decorations like a mechanical songbird, a full-size carousel horse and handpainted wall murals. Disneyland gives away stays in the suite as a **prize** from time to time, so keep your eyes peeled for your chance to win and **good luck!**

Club 33 is a members-only restaurant located above the shops in New Orleans Square. The club gets its name from its address at **33 Royal Street.** To enter, members press a buzzer near a green door which is marked only by the number 33 etched in the glass above. Inside, Guests enjoy gourmet food and cocktails—which are not served anywhere else in the park. Members enjoy other perks too—like instant FastPass tickets to use wherever they like and **free entry** to Disneyland, Disney California Adventure and its private **1901** club—named after the year Walt Disney was born. Think you'd like to become a member? The fee to join is over **$25,000** and the yearly dues are over **$10,000** so...**save your allowance!**

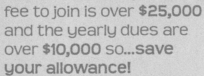

Where would **YOU** rather spend the evening?
☐ Dream Suite
☐ Club 33
Why?

_____

_____

_____

"You know the thing about good food? It brings folks together from all walks of life. It warms them right up and it puts little smiles on their faces."

—JAMES

★ Food & Drinks

Blue Bayou Restaurant

It's always a beautiful evening on the bayou at this elegant, full-service restaurant. Though it's actually all indoors, you'll feel like you're outside on a veranda under a starry sky.

• *Jambalaya* • *Salmon* • *Steak*

 SPY What a view! The **Pirates of the Caribbean boats** float right by the tables of this restaurant.

French Market Restaurant

If your timing is right, you can snag a spot on the shady patio while enjoying wonderful musical performances by the Royal Street Bachelors or Jambalaya Jazz Band.

• *Cajun meatloaf* • *Po' boy sandwiches* • *Red beans & rice*

 HOT TIP At the back of French Market Restaurant is the **Mint Julep Bar,** a walk-up window where beignets and Mint Juleps—are served.

café ORLeans

Choose to sit inside the handsome, wood-paneled dining room or watch the world go by under an umbrella on the patio. The glimmering gold antique espresso machine inside was actually bought by Walt and Lillian Disney.

• *Crêpes* • *Monte Cristo sandwiches*
• *Pommes frites with Cajun rémoulade* • *Ragoût*

Inside the café, check out the oil painting of **Philippe II, Duke of Orléans,** the French nobleman who **New Orleans** was named after.

Royal Street VeRanda

This walk-up window on Royal Street is named for the street on which it sits. All of the lanes in New Orleans Square—Front Street, Orleans Street and Royal Street—are named after streets in the real city of New Orleans, Louisiana.

• *Clam chowder* • *Fritters* • *Gumbo*

Look at the **balcony** above Royal Street Veranda to see the **initials** of Walt Disney and his brother Roy Disney on the railing.

DID YOU EAT IN NEW ORLEANS SQUARE?
☐ Yes ☐ No
If yes, where?
_____
What'd ya have?
_____
_____
_____
Was it good?
☐ Yes ☐ No
☐ Maybe So

Bon appétit! (enjoy your meal)

New Orleans Square's restaurants have some pretty **unique choices** on the menu! Many dishes are **Southern** or **French** style, just like the food that's famously delicious in the **real New Orleans.** Which will you try?

❧ **Beignets**
Airy pastries covered in powdered sugar

❧ **Crêpes**
Thin pancakes with fillings that can be sweet or salty

❧ **Fritters**
Fried dough with dipping sauces

❧ **Gumbo**
A thick stew usually made with chicken or seafood

❧ **Jambalaya**
A spicy dish with rice, meat and veggies

❧ **Monte Cristo sandwiches**
Deep fried turkey, ham and swiss cheese sandwich, dusted with powdered sugar and served with sweet dipping sauce

❧ **Po' boy sandwiches**
Louisiana-style sub sandwich

❧ **Pommes frites**
The name for these thin french fries means "fried potatoes" in French

❧ **Ragoût**
A flavorful stew with meat and/or veggies

❧ **Rémoulade**
A cold sauce made with mayo and herbs

★ # Unique Souvenirs

YOUR VERY OWN GLASS

Choose your glass, and skilled artisans will engrave your name, initials or short message on it at **Cristal d'Orleans** in New Orleans Square or Crystal Arts in Main Street USA.

 The **masters of engraving** working in these shops are so good at what they do, they're fun to **watch** even if you're not buying a thing!

RUFFLED UMBRELLA

Pop by the **Parasol Cart** to peruse the perfect, painted parasols. You can choose to have words, characters, hearts or other designs added— there are lots to choose from!

 The parasols are **hand-painted** and need time to dry. The artist will let you know when it'll be ready to pick up.

PIRATE PEARLS OF WISDOM

Like to get your fortune read? Fortune Red, the red-haired pirate just outside **Pieces of Eight,** is happy to oblige. Insert two quarters and a bit of *Yo Ho (A Pirate's Life for Me)* will play before a card pops out with your fortune on one side and a history of Jolly Roger pirate flags on the other.

anchors away

There's something very peculiar sprouting out of a flowerbed along the banks of the Rivers of America—a rusty, **anchor** covered in barnacles. A sign in front says it's **Lafitte's Anchor** but just who was Lafitte? Jean Lafitte was a **real pirate** who terrorized the waters around Louisiana in the early 1800s. When Louisiana's Governor offered a **$300** reward for his capture, Lafitte played a prank and printed flyers offering a **$1,000** reward if anyone could capture the governor! You'll find the dreaded pirate's name in other spots around Disneyland. The loading platform on Pirates of the Caribbean is named **Laffite's Landing** (with two f's and one t) and a building on Tom Sawyer Island is called **Lafitte's Tavern.** So, was this anchor **really** once the property of the real Jean Lafitte? Don't believe everything you read...

VICIOUS VILLAINS!

Villains! Those cruel, wicked characters that everyone **loves** to hate. Can you match the villain to the **movie** they appeared in? The first one's been done for you. *Answers on page 181.*

Jafar	*Snow White and the Seven Dwarfs*
Ursula	*The Princess and the Frog*
Gaston	*Beauty and the Beast*
Dr. Facilier	*Alice in Wonderland*
Maleficent	*The Little Mermaid*
Cruella de Vil	*Sleeping Beauty*
Captain Hook	*101 Dalmatians*
The Evil Queen	*Peter Pan*
The Queen of Hearts	*Aladdin*

The name of Le Bat en Rouge shop is a clever play on words to sound like Baton Rouge, the capital of Louisiana.

CRITTER COUNTRY

What Will You Find in This Land?

ATTRACTIONS
- Davy Crockett's Explorer Canoes
- The Many Adventures of Winnie the Pooh
- Splash Mountain

FOOD & DRINKS
- Harbour Galley
- Hungry Bear Restaurant

SHOPS
- The Briar Patch
- Pooh Corner
- Professor Barnaby Owl's Photographic Art Studio

MEET N' GREETS
- Winnie the Pooh & Friends

ALSO IN THIS CHAPTER
- Where Do I Work?
- Pooh Primer
- Kitty Critters
- Spot the Dog, Spy the Cat!

KEY

- ⭕ ATTRACTIONS
- ⭕ FOOD & DRINKS
- ⭕ RESTROOMS
- ⭕ SHOPS

THE RIVERS OF AMERICA

RESTROOM

Hungry Bear Restaurant

Davy Crockett's Explorer Canoes

The Many Adventures of Winnie the Pooh

The Briar Patch

Pooh Corner

Splash Mountain

Harbour Galley

Professor Barnaby Owl's Photographic Art Studio

NEW ORLEANS SQUARE ›

SO YOU KNOW...
critter = a country-type word for an animal

BEAR

RABBIT

TOAD

DOG

Waiting Game!

CRITTER CHAIN

In this game for 2 or more players, one player begins by saying the name of an animal. The next player must say the name of an animal that starts with the last letter of that word. If a player can't think of an answer, whoever said the last animal is the winner. You may not say the same word twice but using different names for the same critter is okay—like "bunny" and "rabbit."

Down Home Fun

Critter Country has always looked roughly the same with its woodsy setting and rustic buildings, but it's been through a lot of changes and has actually had three different names! Opening in 1956, Indian Village was in this spot with Native American activities. The area reopened in 1972 as Bear Country—a honey of a place with a brand new E-ticket attraction called Country Bear Jamboree, a musical show put on by bears and other animals. The name of the land changed for the third time to Critter Country in 1988. The shady paths, wooden buildings and grass-roofed log cabin in this land will make you feel like you're out in the country where cute, woodland creatures might scamper by at anytime.

HOT TIP Unlike most of Disneyland's lands which flow into **other sections** of the park, **Critter Country** is a **dead end** so, once you've had your fun, you'll turn around and go back out **the way you came in.**

Fun Fact

In the 1800s, water-filled flumes at sawmills carried logs downhill to train stations. Thrillseekers who rode down these tracks in boats inspired the first log ride, built in 1962 for an amusement park in Texas.

YEEHAW!

"I can't help laughin', Br'er Fox. I just been to my laughin' place."
—BR'ER RABBIT

★ Splash Mountain

LOG FLUME
EST.
1989
WILD & THRILLING

Hop into a hollow log and float along the lazy streams of Chick-A-Pin Hill—also known as Splash Mountain. Once you're inside, you'll drift past a collection of cheerful critters singing *How Do You Do* as spunky **Br'er** Rabbit leaves home in search of his laughin' place. He finds it but mischievous Br'er Bear and Br'er Fox are hot on his trail and manage to trap Br'er Rabbit in a beehive. Things get dark and ominous as the log slowly climbs to the big drop—a five-story, 45-degree angle fall! As a pair of vile vultures snicker overhead, the log plummets down, down, down through the thorny branches and splashes into the water below! After winding around the bend—while trying to see just how wet you got—you'll float past animals aboard a grand riverboat singing Zip-a-Dee-Doo-Dah as Br'er Rabbit kicks back at home, safe and sound.

HOT TIP Your photo is taken right when you go down Splash Mountain's **big drop!** If you want to buy a print, head to **Professor Barnaby Owl's Photographic Art Studio** near the exit of the ride.

Illustration by Steve Willis

TIME MACHINE

1881
"Uncle Remus, His Songs & His Sayings" by Joel Chandler Harris is published.

1946
"Song of the South," based on the Uncle Remus books & starring Br'er Rabbit, hits theaters.

1988
Tomorrowland's America Sings closes & many of its characters relocate to Splash Mountain.

1989
Splash Mountain, based on "Song of the South," welcomes its first riders. Zip-a-Dee-Doo-AHHH!

Fun Facts about Splash Mountain

Splash Mountain is 87 feet high & travels about half a mile from start to finish.

Near the start of the ride you can see—and hear—the cave of Br'er Bear. Imagineers added this to pay tribute to Rufus the Bear, whose cave sat at the entrance to Bear Country before it changed to Critter Country.

The song "Zip-a-Dee-Doo-Dah" won Best Original Song at the 20th Annual Academy Awards in 1948.

Imagineer Tony Baxter thought of the idea for Splash Mountain in 1983 when he was stuck in traffic during his morning commute!

Signs warn you that "You may get wet" but riders on the right side in the back may get LESS wet.

FUN FACT
American fok hero Davy Crockett was born in 1786 & was nicknamed "King of the Wild Frontier." He was a hunter, statesman & was well known for his talent for telling tall tales.

★ Davy Crockett's Explorer Canoes

"Always be sure you are right, then go ahead."
—DAVY CROCKETT

—est.— **1956** OUTDOOR Boat Ride · Lively & exciting ·

What makes these 35-foot canoes go? **YOU!** This is the only attraction that's actually powered by Guests, and one of the few rides that's not on a track. You'll feel just like the real Davy Crockett exploring the wild American frontier as you climb aboard and grab your paddle. Never been in a canoe? Never fear! Your guides will show you just what to do. You'll travel the same route as Mark Twain Riverboat and Sailing Ship Columbia, and paddle all the way around Tom Sawyer Island past many interesting sights and sounds.

HOT TIP The canoes only run **seasonally**, may close in bad weather and are only open during **limited hours** in the daytime.

SPY Each of Davy's canoes has a **different design** on the side. If you ride the canoes, take a look and see which picture is on your canoe!

TIME MACHINE

1836
Crockett is killed in the Battle of the Alamo. Today, the Alamo sells 15,000 coonskin caps a year.

1955
"Davy Crockett, King of the Wild Frontier" hits theaters.

1956
Indian War Canoes open in Disneyland.

1971
Canoes reopen after being renamed after "Da-vy, Da-vy Crockett."

WHERE DO I WORK?

Cast Members wear **outfits** that match the **theme** of the attraction where they work. Can you guess which outfit matches which attraction? Draw a line connecting the outfit to the name of the attraction. The first one's been done for you. *Answers on page 181.*

Davy Crockett's Explorer Canoes

Haunted Mansion

Indiana Jones Adventure

Jungle Cruise

Matterhorn Bobsleds

Pirates of the Caribbean

Where would you like to work if **YOU** worked in Disneyland? Why?

_____

_____

_____

"A day without a friend is like a pot without
a single drop of honey left inside."
—WINNIE THE POOH

MAY BE
SCARY

FUN FaCT

*Imagineers put a
special tribute in the
Winnie the Pooh ride.
Look behind you when
you leave the Heffalumps
& Woozles scene, to see
Max, Buff & Melvin who
used to be in Country
Bear Jamboree
before Winnie
moved in.*

CUTE!

The Many Adventures
of Winnie the Pooh

INDOOR DARK RIDE ★ —EST.— 2003 ★ Lively & exciting

No matter what the weather is outside,
it's a blustery day inside this journey
through the world of Winnie the Pooh.
You'll hop in a beehive and travel through
the Hundred Acre Wood where Pooh
is doing what he usually does—hunting for honey!
After a rainstorm, Pooh falls asleep. As you travel through
his wild dream, you'll see colorful Heffalumps, wacky
Woozles and buzzing Heffabees. After Pooh wakes up,
his friends throw him a big party with balloons, cake,
presents and even a Smackerel of honey!

HOT TIP When you walk through the **Pooh Corner**
shop, take a sniff and see if you can
smell the **honey-scented air!**

★ Meet n' Greets

Head towards the back of Critter Country
to meet Winnie the Pooh & Friends
like Eeyore the Donkey and Tigger the Tiger!

Illustration by Sam Carter • SamCarterArt.com

TIME MACHINE

1924
*A.A. Milne's book of poems
called "When We Were
Very Young" featuring
Christopher Robin &
Pooh is published.*

1932
*Winnie the Pooh is seen
for the first time in his
signature red shirt on the
cover of a record album.*

1966
*"Winnie the Pooh &
the Honey Tree" hits
theaters—the first
of many Winnie the
Pooh movies.*

2003
*The Many Adventures
of Winnie the Pooh
opens. Sweet!*

POOH PRIMER

NAME Christopher Robin
TYPE OF ANIMAL Human
QUOTE "Even if we're apart, I'll always be with you."
HOBBY Visiting the Hundred Acre Wood
PERSONALITY Cheerful, wise

NAME Eeyore
TYPE OF ANIMAL Donkey
QUOTE "I was so upset, I forgot to be happy."
HOBBY Rebuilding his house of sticks
PERSONALITY Glum, negative

NAME Kanga
TYPE OF ANIMAL Kangaroo
QUOTE "Oh, my goodness!"
HOBBY Doting on her son, Roo
PERSONALITY Patient, tidy

NAME Owl
TYPE OF ANIMAL Owl
QUOTE "And now you know the horrible truth!"
HOBBY Telling stories
PERSONALITY Friendly, rambling

NAME Piglet
TYPE OF ANIMAL Piglet
QUOTE "Oh, d-d-dear!"
HOBBY Overcoming his fears
PERSONALITY Gentle, shy

NAME Rabbit
TYPE OF ANIMAL Rabbit
QUOTE "Hmm, I don't see much sense in that."
HOBBY Gardening
PERSONALITY Bossy, irritable

NAME Roo
TYPE OF ANIMAL Kangaroo
QUOTE "Whee!"
HOBBY Playing
PERSONALITY Curious, joyful

NAME Tigger
TYPE OF ANIMAL Tiger
QUOTE "Hoo Hoo Hoo Hoo!"
HOBBY Bouncing
PERSONALITY Energetic, over-confident

NAME Winnie the Pooh
TYPE OF ANIMAL Bear
QUOTE "People say nothing is impossible, but I do nothing every day."
HOBBY Eating honey
PERSONALITY Naive, thoughtful

Kitty Critters

There are many **animals** in Disneyland, like the **horses** who pull the Horse-Drawn Streetcars up and down Main Street and the **ducks** who swim in the Rivers of America. But you may be surprised to learn that Disneyland is also home to lots and lots of **wild kitty cats**! No one is really sure how they got there but Disneyland takes good care of them and likes how they catch pesky **mice** and other rodents—who just aren't as cute as **Mickey**. It is thought that there are around **200** cats in and around the park but it's very rare to actually see one. Since they're wild, they usually stay away from areas where there are lots of people. **Keep your eyes peeled** though and you just might spy one!

Spot the Dog, Spy the Cat!

Disney movies are full of cat and dog characters! Write a "C" by each Disney **cat** and a "D" next to each Disney **dog** in the list below. The first two have been done for you. *Answers on page 181.*

[D] Bruno from *Cinderella*

[C] Cheshire Cat from *Alice in Wonderland*

[ ] Figaro from *Pinocchio*

[ ] Lady from *Lady and the Tramp*

[ ] Lucifer from *Cinderella*

[ ] Marie from *The Aristocats*

[ ] Max from *The Little Mermaid*

[ ] Nana from *Peter Pan*

[ ] Pongo from *101 Dalmatians*

[ ] Rajah from *Aladdin*

[ ] Shere Khan from *The Jungle Book*

[ ] Simba from *The Lion King*

[ ] Tigger from *Winnie the Pooh*

[ ] Zero from *The Nightmare Before Christmas*

LADY

> "What could be more important than a little something to eat?"
> —WINNIE THE POOH

Food & Drinks

Hungry Bear Restaurant

Saunter across a wooden bridge to this rustic, woodsy spot with two stories of decks overlooking the sights and sounds of the Rivers of America.

- *Chicken sandwiches* • *Funnel cake*
- *Hamburgers* • *Onion rings*

SPY

Do you like to see choo-choos while you chew? Head up to the **second story** of this restaurant to the left of the ordering counters to watch the **Disneyland Railroad** trains steam by.

Harbour Galley

Grab a bite at this nautical New England–style eatery, find a spot on the pier and enjoy views of the hustle and bustle of the Rivers of America.

- *Clam chowder* • *Lobster rolls* • *Tuna sandwiches*

SPY

Keep walking past the **outdoor tables** of Harbour Galley and up a short staircase to find a **secret path.** You'll have great views of Splash Mountain's smiling riders fresh off the **big drop!**

Mini Quiz!

A kitchen on a ship is called a "galley." Can you guess what a ship's bathroom is called?
Answer on page 181.

☐ Head   ☐ Port

☐ Rudder   ☐ Starboard

DID YOU EAT IN CRITTER COUNTRY?

☐ Yes   ☐ No
If yes, where?

_____

What'd ya have?

_____

_____

_____

Was it good?
☐ Yes   ☐ No
☐ Maybe So

FUN FACT

Along the path near Harbour Galley, a sign reads "Fowler's Inn." This sign & one inside Splash Mountain honor retired Admiral Joe Fowler. He gave advice on how to build Mark Twain Riverboat & ended up working for the Disney Company for over 20 years.

SUPER!

Look for this cute Br'er Rabbit wishing well as you frolic through Critter Country!

Micky

33

My Trip Journal

TASW

Fantasyland

MR. Bluebird's House

CRITTER COUNTRY

HAUNTED MANSION
NEW ORLEANS SQUARE
FRIGHTENINGLY FUN!

MAIN STREET USA
We'll Leave the Light on for you

WE'RE NUTS ABOUT TOONTOWN
Micky's

TOMORROWLAND
TO INFINITY AND BEYOND!

DARE NOT GAZE UPON THE EYES OF MARA
ADVENTURELAND

LIVIN' A BLAST!
FRONTIERLAND

PROPERTY OF:

....

My TRiP JouRNaL-about My Visit

Date(s) of visit to Disneyland: ....

How many days were you there? ....

Who did you go with? ....

How was the weather? ....

Did you go to Disney California Adventure? ☐ Yes ☐ No

Did you go to Downtown Disney? ☐ Yes ☐ No

Draw a picture of yourself in Disneyland:

My TRiP JOuRNaL—aBOut My ViSit

Which land did you like best?

☐ Adventureland ☐ Critter Country ☐ Fantasyland
☐ Frontierland ☐ Main Street USA ☐ New Orleans Square
☐ Tomorrowland ☐ Mickey's Toontown

Why was it your favorite land? . . . .

. . . .

What was the best attraction of all? . . . .

Was there anything you wanted to do but couldn't? Why?

. . . .

. . . .

What was the most delicious thing you ate or drank? . . . .

. . . .

Did you see any shows when you were there? If so, what did you see?

. . . .

. . . .

Did you see any characters when you were there? If so, which ones?

. . . .

. . . .

. . . .

. . . .

MY TRIP JOURNAL-SCRAPBOOK

When you're visiting Disneyland hold on to receipts, napkins, maps, stickers, admission tickets, PhotoPass cards, unused FastPass tickets, handouts from City Hall and other flat things to tape or glue onto these pages.

My Trip Journal-Scrapbook

MY TRIP JOURNAL-SCRAPBOOK

My Trip Journal—Autographs

Characters in Disneyland love to meet their fans and give autographs! Collect character autographs and stamps here.

Don't be shy.
Even villains
love to meet
their fans!

Write a pretend postcard to your favorite Disney character about your visit to Disneyland!

Going To Guides
www.GoingToGuides.com
Going To Disneyland

To:
_____
_____
_____

Want to write to us too? We'd love to hear from you!
Write to Going To Guides at:
PO Box 217 • Lafayette, CA 94549
www.GoingToGuides.com
Mailroom@GoingToGuides.com

Super, Super-Short Stories

Visiting Disneyland can be more fun when you know and love Disney characters and stories. Here are some short versions of many of the stories you'll experience and where you'll see them in the park.

Alice in Wonderland

Sitting with her sister on a riverbank, Alice sees a White Rabbit and is curious where he's headed. Following him, she falls down a hole into a strange place called Wonderland. She eats and drinks things that make her grow larger and smaller, and can't get a straight answer from any of the wacky characters she meets along the way—like Tweedle Dee, Tweedle Dum, the Cheshire Cat, and the Caterpillar. After a crazy tea party with the Mad Hatter, the March Hare and the Doormouse, Alice decides she's ready to go home but gets lost in Tulgey Wood. When the Queen of Hearts orders "Off with her head," Alice escapes at last and wakes up back on the riverbank.

ATTRACTIONS: Alice in Wonderland • Mad Tea Party
SHOPS: The Mad Hatter (2 locations)

Dumbo

As the Casey Jr. Circus Train arrives in town, a circus elephant named Mrs. Jumbo gets a visit from Mr. Stork who brings her a baby boy. She is delighted with her new child and names him Jumbo, Jr. but the other animals make fun of his huge ears and call him Dumbo. When some mean kids tease her son, Mrs. Jumbo goes into a rage and is locked up. The little elephant is very sad without his mother but makes friends with a little mouse named Timothy Q. Mouse. After a wild night, Timothy and Dumbo wake up in a tall tree and Timothy guesses that Dumbo must have flown them up there. To boost Dumbo's confidence in himself, he gives him a magic feather and tells Dumbo that if he has that, he'll be able to fly. Dumbo believes in the magic, flaps his ears and takes off into the air. Later, when performing at the circus, Dumbo loses the feather and realizes he never needed it to fly anyway. Dumbo becomes famous for his flying skills and is reunited with his beloved mother at last!

ATTRACTIONS: Casey Jr. Circus Train • Dumbo the Flying Elephant
FOOD & DRINKS: Dumbo Churro Cart

Finding Nemo

A cautious clownfish named Marlin living in Australia's Great Barrier Reef is overly protective of his son Nemo. When Nemo is caught and put in an aquarium in a dentist's office, Marlin sets off to find him and bring him home. A forgetful blue tang fish named Dory joins Marlin in the search—though most of the time she doesn't remember what she's doing or what just happened! Marlin and Dory meet three sharks named Bruce, Anchor and Chum who are trying to be nicer by living by the motto, "Fish are friends, not food." After escaping from a terrifying deep-sea anglerfish and beautiful but dangerous jellyfish, Marlin and Dory are shown how to ride the EAC—or East Australian Current—by Crush the Turtle and his son Squirt. Meanwhile Nemo and his new friends in the fish tank learn that Nemo is going to be given to the dentist's daughter Darla, a little girl who has already killed a fish by shaking the bag it was in. Nemo manages to escape from the fish tank and get back to the ocean where he is finally reunited with his dad.

ATTRACTION: Finding Nemo Submarine Voyage

King Arthur

A mysterious sword appears in London with an inscription which states that whoever can remove it from the anvil that it's stuck in will become King. Years later, a young boy named Arthur, who was given an unusual education from a wizard called Merlin, easily removes the sword without even knowing that it's special. Now King of England, Arthur is not sure that he's up for the job but Merlin tells him he'll become one of the most famous Kings in literature.

ATTRACTION: King Arthur Carrousel

Mary Poppins

Mary Poppins saves the day for the Banks family when she floats down from the sky with an umbrella to become Jane and Michael Banks' nanny. As Mrs. Banks goes off to fight for a woman's right to vote, Mary takes the children on an outing where they meet her friend Bert who's working as a sidewalk artist. They all jump into one of his chalk drawings where they ride carousel horses through an animated countryside and Bert sings and dances for Mary with a group of penguin waiters. Later Mary, Bert and the children visit Uncle Albert for tea and find that he has laughed so much, he's floated up to the ceiling. The laughter is contagious and soon they all join him up in the air. Back at home, Mr. Banks disapproves of the children's stories and Mary tricks him into taking them to the bank where he works. When Michael wants to spend a tuppence coin to feed the birds, he creates a panic at the bank and Mr. Banks ends up being fired from his job. When their father realizes he was being too severe with Jane and Michael and helps them with their kite, Mary knows her job is done, opens her umbrella and flies away.

ATTRACTION: King Arthur Carrousel
FOOD & DRINKS: Jolly Holiday Bakery Café

MR. TOAD

James Thaddeus Toad loves to drive his cart around the countryside like a maniac with his horse Cyril Proudbottom. His friends Angus MacBadger, Ratty and Moley try to get him to settle down and take care of his estate, Toad Hall, but instead he goes to Mr. Winky's Tavern and trades Toad Hall away to a gang of weasels in return for a newfangled motorcar. Mr. Toad is accused of stealing the car and sent to jail. At his trial, Mr. Toad is found guilty and sentenced to twenty years in the Tower of London. Cyril helps his friend escape from jail and win back ownership of Toad Hall.

ATTRACTION: Mr. Toad's Wild Ride

Peter Pan

Mr. Darling gets jealous that Mrs. Darling and their children, Wendy, Michael and John, are making a bigger fuss over Nana the Dog than they are of him. He orders Nana outside and tells Wendy it's time for her to grow up and that this will be her last night with her brothers in the nursery. Wendy tries to tell her mother that Peter Pan has been visiting the nursery and she's captured his shadow, but her mother doesn't listen. After Mr. and Mrs. Darling go out for the evening, Peter and his fairy friend Tinker Bell fly in the window to find Peter's shadow. Peter sprinkles the three children with Tinker Bell's pixie dust, tells them to think happy thoughts and flies with them back to Never Land—a wondrous place where children never grow up. Never Land is home to the Lost Boys, beautiful mermaids, Native American Indian princess Tiger Lily and her father the Indian Chief, pirate Captain Hook and his faithful assistant Mr. Smee, and hungry crocodile Tick-Tock—named for the ticking clock he accidentally swallowed. Peter had fed Hook's hand to the croc and he's been eager to get another taste of him ever since. Wendy, John, Michael and the Lost Boys realize they miss their mother and want to go home but are captured by the pirates. After Hook gets Tinker Bell to reveal Peter's location, he delivers a bomb to Peter, now alone in his secret hideout. Tink saves Peter but almost dies in the explosion. She and Peter defeat the pirates, Hook is chased into the distance by Tick-Tock, and Peter takes the Darling children home in a flying pirate ship that their father could swear he's seen somewhere before.

ATTRACTION: Peter Pan's Flight
MEET N' GREETS: Tinker Bell and Fairy Friends

Pinocchio

The woodcarver Geppetto makes a puppet named Pinocchio and wishes he were alive. The Blue Fairy makes him come to life but tells him he can never be a real boy until he learns to be brave, truthful and unselfish. She asks Jiminy Cricket to be his conscience and help him learn the difference between right and wrong. Pinocchio is supposed to go to school but lets Honest John the Fox and Gideon the Cat convince him to work in Stromboli's puppet theatre. Pinocchio becomes the star of the show but, when he wants to go home, Stromboli locks him in a birdcage. Pinocchio promises to be good so the Blue Fairy frees him. On his way home, he runs into Honest John and Gideon again, who convince him that he needs to take a vacation on Pleasure Island. Pinocchio makes friends with a boy named Lampwick and the two discover the island is cursed and turns naughty children into donkeys. Lampwick isn't so lucky but Pinocchio escapes with only a donkey's ears and tail. When he gets home, he finds out Geppetto has gone to look for him and has been swallowed by Monstro the Whale. When Pinocchio rushes off and bravely and unselfishly saves Geppetto, the Blue Fairy decides that he has proven that he should be turned into a real boy.

ATTRACTIONS: Pinocchio's Daring Journey • Storybook Land Canal Boats
FOOD & DRINKS: Village Haus Restaurant

Sleeping Beauty

King Stefan and Queen Leah are overjoyed at the birth of their daughter Aurora and make arrangements for her to marry Prince Phillip when she grows up. Three good fairies named Flora, Fauna and Merryweather come to bless the princess but are interrupted by the evil fairy Maleficent who is angry that she wasn't invited. She puts a curse on the princess and says that, before the end of her sixteenth birthday, she will prick her finger on the spindle of a spinning wheel and die. Merryweather has yet to give her blessing so she uses it to lessen the curse, saying that, instead of dying, Aurora will fall into a sleep that can be broken by true love's kiss. The three fairies take the princess and hide her in a cottage in the woods where they call her Briar Rose. On her sixteenth birthday, Aurora meets and falls in love with Prince Phillip, not knowing that she's already engaged to marry him. Meanwhile the prince tries to convince his father to let him marry the peasant girl he met in the woods. The three fairies take Aurora back to her father's castle where Maleficent lures her to prick her finger on a spinning wheel and fall into a deep sleep. The fairies cast a spell making everyone in the castle fall asleep until Prince Phillip defeats Maleficent, finds Aurora, kisses her and breaks the curse.

ATTRACTIONS: Sleeping Beauty Castle Walkthrough • King Arthur Carrousel

Snow White and the Seven Dwarfs

As the princess Snow White sweetly sings by a wishing well, a handsome prince joins her in song and they fall in love. But Snow White's villainous stepmother, the Evil Queen, is jealous of her beauty and orders her huntsman to take Snow White out to the forest to kill her and bring back her heart. The huntsman can't bring himself to do it and tells Snow White to run away into the woods where she finds the cottage of the seven dwarfs—Bashful, Doc, Dopey, Grumpy, Happy, Sleepy and Sneezy. The dwarfs mine for jewels all day and agree to let Snow White stay with them in exchange for cooking and cleaning their cottage. Meanwhile, the Evil Queen learns from her Magic Mirror that Snow White is still alive and that the heart the huntsman brought her was just a pig's heart. The Evil Queen disguises herself as an Old Hag, visits Snow White and tricks her into tasting a poisoned apple. Snow White fall into a sleeping death that can only be broken by true love's kiss. The dwarfs return and chase the Evil Queen up a cliff where she is struck by lightning and falls to her death. When the dwarfs return to their cottage and see Snow White, they think she's dead and place her in a glass coffin. The prince comes to pay his respects and everyone is surprised and overjoyed when his kiss awakens her.

ATTRACTIONS: Snow White Grotto • Snow White's Scary Adventures

Tarzan

A baby boy's parents are killed by a ferocious leopard named Sabor in the jungle. A gorilla couple named Kerchak and Kala, who lost their own baby to Sabor, raise him as one of their own and name him Tarzan. As Tarzan grows up, he makes friends with Terk the Gorilla and Tantor the Elephant. A group of explorers from England come to the island including Professor Porter, his daugher Jane and a hunter named Clayton. After Tarzan saves Jane from a pack of baboons, she takes him back to the camp where everyone is fascinated by him. The Professor and Jane teach Tarzan about the human world, and Tarzan and Jane fall in love. Clayton tricks Tarzan into telling him where the gorillas are so he can capture them. After battling Kerchak and Tarzan, Clayton ends up falling to his death. As Kerchak dies from his wounds, he tells Tarzan that he is now the leader of the gorillas. When the professor and Jane get on a boat to leave the island, Tarzan tells them he plans to stay with his animal friends. Jane jumps overboard to be with him followed soon after by her father.

ATTRACTION: Tarzan's Treehouse

Toy Story

Sheriff Woody, Mr. Potato Head, Hamm the Piggy Bank, Rex the Dinosaur, Slinky Dog, Bo Peep and the rest of the toys belong to a little boy named Andy and come to life when people aren't around. The toys welcome a new spaceman action figure called Buzz Lightyear to Andy's Room but soon discover he thinks he's a real astronaut and doesn't know he's a toy! When Buzz ends up at the neighbor's house, he sees a commercial for a Buzz Lightyear action figure and is depressed to realize that he's just a toy. Woody convinces him being a toy is actually a good thing and together they escape and make it back home. Later, when Woody is taken by a vintage toy collector, Buzz and some other toys go to rescue him and end up at a toy store where they encounter a Zurg toy. This evil Emporer from the Buzz Lightyear universe thinks *he's* real and tries to destroy Buzz. Just in the nick of time, Buzz and the other toys free Woody and his new friends Bullseye and Jessie.

ATTRACTION: Buzz Lightyear Astro Blasters
SHOP: Little Green Men Store Command

Who Framed Roger Rabbit

Roger Rabbit stars in cartoons with cigar-chomping Baby Herman and lives in Toontown where cartoon characters—or "Toons"—live. A down-and-out detective named Eddie Valiant is hired to look into rumors about Roger's wife, Jessica Rabbit. Eddie thinks she'll be a rabbit like Roger but that's just her married name. She's actually a beautiful songstress who performs at the Ink & Paint Club. When Roger is accused of a crime he didn't commit, he turns to Valiant for help. Valiant hates Toons but senses something's rotten in Toontown. He wants to get to the bottom of it and agrees to help Roger. Judge Doom and his Toon Patrol of corrupt weasels are on the hunt for Roger armed with deadly Dip—a toxic mixture of chemicals deadly to Toons. Roger and Valiant manage to escape with the help of Benny the Cab. Valiant ends up discovering and stopping a scheme to destroy Toontown and realizes that maybe Toons aren't so bad after all.

ATTRACTION: Roger Rabbit's Car Toon Spin

Winnie the Pooh

A little boy named Christopher Robin has adventures in Hundred Acre Wood with his honey-loving teddy bear Winnie the Pooh and other toys Eeyore, Piglet, Tigger, Owl, Rabbit, Kanga and her son Roo. Strange creatures appear in Winnie the Pooh's dreams—Heffalumps that look sort of like elephants, Woozles that look sort of like weasels and Heffabees that look like a cross between a Heffalump and a honeybee.

ATTRACTION: The Many Adventures of Winnie the Pooh
MEET N' GREETS: Winnie the Pooh & Friends
SHOP: Pooh Corner

Game Answers

PAGE 17—Phony Baloney!
The Beast's Beauty Shop

PAGE 28—Say What?
"He's no monster, Gaston—you are!" = Belle
"Do you trust me?" = Aladdin
"The human world...it's a mess!" = Sebastian the Crab
"Frying pans. Who knew, right?" = Flynn Rider
"Some people are worth melting for" = Olaf

PAGE 51—Who Shops Where?
Belle = Beastly Books; Cinderella = The Glass Slipper; Genie = Lamps R-Us; Minnie Mouse = Bow Boutique; Rapunzel = Kingdom of Corona Lanterns; Pinocchio = Real Boy Clothing; Cruella de Vil = Fabulous Furs; Olaf = Arendelle Snowman Supplies; Winnie the Pooh = The Hunny Pot; Ariel = Dinglehoppers

PAGE 59—What's in a Name?
Bashful; Doc; Sleepy; Dopey; Grumpy; Happy; Sneezy

PAGE 61—Boat Name Scrambles!
Faline; Wendy; Daisy; Alice; Cinderella; Belle; Flower; Aurora; Katrina; Snow White; Tinker Bell; Ariel; Flora, Fauna & Merryweather

PAGE 68—Mini Quiz!
Jumbo, Jr.

PAGE 79—Guess the Coat of Arms!
Elsa; Captain Hook; Gaston

PAGE 90—Mini Quiz!
Clarabelle

PAGE 99—Star Wars Character Quiz!
Clockwise from top left: Luke Skywalker; Darth Vader; R2-D2; C-3PO; Stormtrooper; Yoda; Han Solo; Chewbacca

PAGE 101—Mini Quiz!
Richard Nixon

PAGE 104—Mini Quiz!
Sneeze

PAGE 116—Mini Quiz!
Snakes

PAGE 117—Decode the Secret Message!
Cavern of Bubbling Death

PAGE 132—Mini Quiz!
River Belle Terrace

PAGE 149—Vicious Villains!
Jafar = *Aladdin*
Ursula = *The Little Mermaid*
Gaston = *Beauty and the Beast*
Dr. Facilier = *The Princess and the Frog*
Maleficent = *Sleeping Beauty*
Cruella de Vil = *101 Dalmatians*
Captain Hook = *Peter Pan*
The Evil Queen = *Snow White and the Seven Dwarfs*
The Queen of Hearts = *Alice in Wonderland*

PAGE 157—Where Do I Work?
Clockwise from top left: Davy Crockett's Explorer Canoes; Matterhorn Bobsleds; Indiana Jones Adventure; Pirates of the Caribbean; Jungle Cruise; Haunted Mansion

PAGE 160—Spot the Dog, Spy the Cat!
Bruno = Dog
Cheshire Cat = Cat
Figaro = Cat
Lady = Dog
Lucifer = Cat
Marie = Cat
Max = Dog
Nana = Dog
Pongo = Dog
Rajah = Cat
Shere Khan = Cat
Simba = Cat
Tigger = Cat
Zero = Dog

PAGE 161—Mini Quiz!
Head

Heartfelt Thanks

This book wouldn't be what it is today without the help of SO many people! Of course I have to thank my parents for my wonderful childhood, for being the Best Parents Ever and for taking me on my first trip to Disneyland. I have now almost totally forgiven you for not taking any photos of me that day. ;-)

Thank you to my oldest son Edward for inspiring me to write this book in the first place and to my youngest son Clark who, now 9 years old, was my "#1 Tester" to make sure it was kid friendly by the time I got around to writing it. I'm also so thankful for the support of my darling husband who listened to me blather on so much about this book that he deserves a medal! Thanks also to my talented brother, THE Steve Willis, who helped me fill this book with wonderful art.

Thank you (in no particular order) to the dear friends who helped me research, brainstorm, fact check and more—effervescent Elizabeth Lewis Cross, ever-chic Kim Carpenter, clever Jason Weesner, fun-loving Stacie Smith, eagle-eyed Thomas Dobrowolski and enthusiastic Summer Albin. Thanks to sweet Laura LeMoine and the always well-coiffed Jennifer Gonzales for digging through their vintage photo collections for me, and to Toni Morris for running her phone battery down and jumping over ropes to take reference photos because she'll do anything for a friend.

Huge thanks go to photographer Dave DeCaro. The look of this book went to a whole new level when Dave's beautiful photos were added. Thank you to all of the amazingly talented artists who let me show off their incredible artwork—especially Kirsten Ulve, J. Shari Ewing and Original Imagineer Rolly Crump who all created pieces specifically for this book. Wait, did I just say Rolly Crump drew a picture for this book?! I'm still pinching myself over that one!

I also have to thank Rolly and his lovely wife Marie for introducing me to Orchard Hill Press who were good enough to put up with all my unbridled enthusiasm. I loved working with their amazing team including the mad genius Hugh Allison (www.hughallison.com) who cared about making every single detail of this book exactly right just as much as I did. Thank you also to Hugh's impressive network of experts—Haunted Mansion consultant Nick Barbera, ragtime consultant Robert Glenn, Disney vehicle consultant Bob Gurr, Walt Disney quote consultant VJ Hicks, Spanish language consultant (and cousin) Nezda Leigh and, of course, his mum Sylvia Allison. While I'm on the topic of Orchard Hill Press, thank you to fellow OHP author Jeff Heimbuch who might just be the nicest guy ever. Jeff, with his finger on the pulse of the park, was always happy to answer my various random questions that I just knew he'd know the answer to.

I'd also like to give a virtual high five to the Disneyland fans who posted thousands of random photos of every square inch of the park so I could double-check details even though I was miles away in the San Francisco Bay Area.

Finally, I have to acknowledge and thank **YOU** for buying this book and holding it in your hot little hands right now even reading the boring Heartfelt Thanks page. You'll never know how much fun I had creating this book for you!

xoxo,
Shannon

Feeling social? Connect with Going To Guides!

@GoingToGuides • www.GoingToGuides.com

Art Credits

All photos without rounded corners or frames are courtesy of
The Going to Disneyland Official Photographer, Dave DeCaro.
To see more of Dave's work, visit http://davelandweb.com

Throughout this book, all photos and illustrations without
a credit are by author Shannon W. Laskey.

Illustrations by contributing artists are given a credit on the page on which they
appear and are listed below as well. Many images are available for purchase
as fine art prints or on other products for resale. Support your
favorite artists—and be sure to tell them you saw them here!

CONTRIBUTING ARTISTS:

Mary Blair
The Bandstand & Mary Blair photo, pg. 45
Images courtesy of the Mary Blair Estate.
To see more of Mary's work,
visit www.MagicOfMaryBlair.com

Chris Buchholz
Main Street vehicles, pg. 43
To see more of Chris' work,
visit www.etsy.com/shop/BuchWorks

Sam Carter
Demon from Mr. Toad's Wild Ride, pg. 66
Trophy heads, pg. 158
Kawaii map of Disneyland, pg. 186
To see more of Sam's work,
visit SamCarterArt.com

Scott Cocking
Tiki god, pg. 112
Shrunken Ned, elephant & coins, pg. 120
To see more of Scott's work,
visit www.SideShowDesign.com

Rolly Crump
Caricature & man-eating plant, pg. 121
To see more of Rolly's work,
visit www.RolandCrump.com

J. Shari Ewing
Never Land, pg. 62
Captain's Quarters, pg. 141
To see more of Shari's work,
visit www.jshariewingart.com

Lindsay Gibson
Poison apple felt pin, pg. 58
Abominable snowman, pg. 77
Tiger & Dole Whip, pg. 119
Doom buggy, pg. 144
To see more of Lindsay's work,
visit www.etsy.com/shop/emandsprout

Marisa Lerin
Round date stamps, various pages
To see more of Marisa's work,
visit www.pixelscrapper.com

Adrian Mentus
Star Wars outfits, pg. 99
To see more of Adrian's work,
visit www.society6.com/ese51

Heather Mettra
Sleeping Beauty Castle, pg. 57
To see more of Heather's work,
visit www.etsy.com/shop/HeatherMettra

Kolby Ratigan
Big Thunder Mountain Railroad model, pg. 129
To see more of Kolby's work,
visit www.kolbykonnection.com

Kirsten Ulve
It's a Small World, pg. 75
To see more of Kirsten's work,
visit www.KirstenUlve.com

W. Jason Weesner
President Lincoln, pg. 42

Steve Willis
Chapter intros, various pages; Jingles, pg. 67;
Congo Queen, pg. 114; Sailing Ship Columbia,
pg. 127; Coonskin cap, pg. 134; Professor Owl,
pg. 154; Hungry Bear lantern, pg. 161; Train
station, pg. 174

If you are an artist and would like to
contribute art to a Going To Guide, stop
by **www.GoingToGuides.com** today!

Index

The Don't-Be-Bored Game!

Turn the page to play a
board game that's **almost** as
much fun as going to Disneyland!

Here's What You Do

GETTING STARTED
For the game pieces, use anything you can
find—coins, LEGO pieces, pebbles, etc.
Just be sure you can tell the pieces apart from each
other and that they are small enough to fit on the spaces.
You will need one dice or a set of numbered
papers (see yellow box below) to play.

HOW TO PLAY
Place game pieces on the START space.
To see who goes first, roll the dice or pick a numbered paper,
and have the person with the highest number begin.
After their turn, the play continues clockwise.
Each player moves their game piece the number of spaces
they roll or pick, following any instructions
on the spaces where they land.

HOW TO WIN
You must get the exact number to land on the last space.
If your number is over the number you need, stay
where you are and try again on your next turn.
The first player to reach the last space
and enjoy the fireworks wins!

TURN THE PAGE TO PLAY!

NO DICE? HERE'S HOW TO MAKE A SET OF NUMBERED PAPERS
Get six small pieces of paper that are all about the same size.
Number each paper from 1 to 6, fold them
up and place them in a hat or bowl.
When it's your turn, pick a paper without peeking
and move the number of spaces it says—1, 2, 3, 4, 5 or 6.
Refold the paper and put it back with the others.

1   2   3   4   5   6

CRITTER COUNTRY

GRAB A LEMONADE AT THE HARBOUR GALLEY.

DAVY CROCKETT'S EXPLORER CANOES CLOSED. GO BACK 3 SPACES.

TAKE A PLUNGE ON SPLASH MOUNTAIN.

MEET WINNIE THE POOH & GET HIS AUTOGRAPH.

WATCH THE CANDY-MAKERS IN POOH CORNER.

PICK UP A FASTPASS FOR SPLASH MOUNTAIN. JUMP AHEAD 5 SPACES.

BOARD A DOOM BUGGY IN THE HAUNTED MANSION.

CATCH A TRAIN TO THE FIRST SPACE IN MICKEY'S TOONTOWN.

DRINK A MINT JULEP. SUGAR RUSH! JUMP AHEAD 2 SPACES.

NO LINE FOR PIRATES OF THE CARIBBEAN. RIDE IT TWICE.

EXPLORE TARZAN'S TREEHOUSE.

HAVE A BALL ON INDIANA JONES ADVENTURE.

PICK UP A FASTPASS FOR INDIANA JONES ADVENTURE. JUMP AHEAD 1 SPACE.

NEW ORLEANS SQUARE

FRONTIERLAND

RIDE THE RAILS ON BIG THUNDER MOUNTAIN RAILROAD.

ENJOY LUNCH AT BIG THUNDER RANCH BARBECUE.

TAKE A CRUISE ON THE MARK TWAIN RIVERBOAT.

HAVE A ROOTIN' TOOTIN' TIME AT THE SHOOTIN' EXPOSITION.

RESTROOM BREAK. LOSE A TURN.

MEET A PRINCESS AT THE ROYAL HALL IN FANTASY FAIRE.

SING LIKE THE BIRDIES SING IN THE TIKI ROOM.

POKE AROUND ADVENTURELAND BAZAAR.

ADVENTURELAND

CRUISE THE JUNGLE WITH A VERY FUNNY SKIPPER.

FANTASYLAND

IS THAT MARY POPPINS ON THE CARROUSEL? JUMP AHEAD 2 SPACES.

SOAR THROUGH THE AIR ON THE DUMBO RIDE.

SPOT CATERPILLAR IN THE MIRROR AT THE MAD HATTER.

TAKE A SPIN IN THE PURPLE CUP ON THE MAD TEA PARTY.

MOTOR THROUGH MR. TOAD'S WILD RIDE.

YOU CAN FLY ON PETER PAN'S FLIGHT.

NO WAIT FOR PINOCCHIO'S DARING JOURNEY. JUMP AHEAD 2 SPACES.

TOUCH THE APPLE IN FRONT OF SNOW WHITE'S SCARY ADVENTURES.

LONG LINE FOR PETER PAN'S FLIGHT. TRY AGAIN LATER.

CATCH A SHOW AT THE ROYAL THEATRE.

MEET MICKEY & MINNIE BY THEIR HOUSES.

ZIP & ZOOM ON GADGET'S GO COASTER.

RING THE BELL ON DONALD'S BOAT.

RESTROOM BREAK. LOSE A TURN.

MICKEY'S TOONTOWN

CATCH A TRAIN TO THE FIRST SPACE IN TOMORROWLAND.

SET SAIL ON IT'S A SMALL WORLD.

GRAB A BITE AT EDELWEISS SNACKS.

DECIDE TO CATCH A TRAIN INSTEAD. GO BACK 3 SPACES.

SPOT THE ABOMINABLE SNOWMAN ON THE MATTERHORN BOBSLEDS.

CENTRAL PLAZA

Main Street USA

GET HOT CHOCOLATE AT MARKET HOUSE.

RESTROOM BREAK. LOSE A TURN.

RIDE ON OMNIBUS. JUMP AHEAD TO CENTRAL PLAZA.

TOMORROWLAND

TAKE A DIVE ON THE FINDING NEMO SUBS.

PICK UP A FASTPASS FOR SPACE MOUNTAIN. JUMP AHEAD 3 SPACES.

GET A HIGH SCORE ON THE BUZZ RIDE. JUMP AHEAD 2 SPACES.

TRAVEL THROUGH OUTER SPACE ON STAR TOURS.

HAVE A BLAST ON SPACE MOUNTAIN.

START

FORGOT THE TICKETS! GO BACK TO START.

ENTER DISNEYLAND & TAKE A PHOTO BY MICKEY FLOWERS.

CATCH A TRAIN TO THE FIRST SPACE IN NEW ORLEANS SQUARE.

TOWN SQUARE

FIREWORKS

CPSIA information can be obtained
at www.ICGtesting.com
Printed in the USA
LVOW06s0552060416

482274LV00016BA/57/P